Introduction

HOLIDAYS: THE MOST RESTORATIVE and uplifting time of the year, when one can enjoy quality time with those you hold dearest, celebrate life and be grateful for the one thing that makes us happiest of all – family. Sorry, alcohol.

Yes, ever since Joseph decided to set off for a (West) Bank Holiday with a heavily pregnant wife and a bafflingly optimistic approach to hotel booking, the family holiday has been a source of biblical proportions of stress. Family holidays are a whirlwind of bitter recriminations, tantrums, road rage and the occasional excruciating bout of casual racism. And that's just on the way to the airport. It's the time you've most likely contemplated murdering a loved one. We might think our love is unconditional, but all it takes is watching them argue with a taxi driver about which is the quickest way to a trattoria in a town they have never visited before, and we all start fantasising about holding them face

down in a poorly serviced hotel swimming pool, before going back to that charming little vineyard we've driven past three times now to dig a shallow grave. A bad trip settles somewhere between a Shakespearian tragedy in flip-flops and a touring version of *The Jeremy Kyle Show*. There will be tears, treachery and possibly the need to go and sit down with a counsellor at the end of it. Surviving such a trip is a balance of mental fortitude and experience. There isn't much I can do to help you with the former, but I decided to write this book at least to impart my wealth of knowledge to help with the latter. It is, I feel, my duty.

Unfortunately, as is the recurring pattern in my life, my parents have decided that it might be helpful if they were to chip in and give you the benefit of their knowledge too. In much the same way that I'm told serial killers eventually feel a desperate need to sit down and confess to their many, many crimes. Using the platform I have unwittingly provided them with, they will dish out their own received wisdom, once again maximising every moment of fame they can get out of their brief time in the sun, like a pair of wizened Love Islanders on statins. I tried to tell them their involvement with this book wasn't necessary and that the objective was to give counsel to my young and vibrant fan base, but my father insisted it would appeal to the older reader as well, the more mature and sophisticated followers he has helped me garner. Quite frankly, I don't have the energy to discourage him any more. He has grown too strong. With each selfie in Waitrose, each appearance in *Countdown*'s 'Dictionary Corner', he grows stronger while I, his host, weaken: a once prodigious young starlet, gradually worn down and reduced to being the sidekick of an eighty-year-old Brexiteer

with intermittent gout. In truth, he acts more and more like the vampire which (let's be honest) he has long physically resembled. By the way, there will be a lot of references to gout in this book. I genuinely think there might be books about Henry VIII that are less 'gouty'. Anyway, it's important to know the context before reading this book, as it wasn't always like this: there was a time when we were just a normal family. Well, normal-ish.

If you're worried that any of this sounds a bit dry, there is also a drinking game that can be played alongside this book. Every time my father drops a name, you knock back a drink. It will have you pissed by about Chapter Four. If you drink double every time the name dropped is a random actor from the seventies you've never heard of, by the end of the book you will be a confused, unemployed alcoholic, possibly like most of the actors he's name-dropped, having endured decades of associating with my father! Go through the whole thing a couple more times, and you'll start to understand what it must be like, on a daily basis, to be Michael Whitehall's liver.

It's also worth mentioning that as well as advice, there will be a fair amount of dirty laundry aired in these pages, having managed to turn this into a kind of family industry. And as is the pitfall of having not one, but three unreliable narrators, there will, I'm sure, be a fair bit of 'remembering it differently'. My father tends to think I overdramatise things. I tend to think his version of our family history involves a kind of North Korean censorship, suppressing the truth in order to paint himself in a better light – namely as a loving father with an impeccable temperament and not some kind of ranting, Dickensian villain in a three-piece suit. However,

I will try my best to tell it like it is – or like it was. I want this book to fall somewhere between Bill Bryson and *A Child Called It*. Travelogue Misery Lit: a whole new genre. I also intend to use as many words as possible that will trigger my father. This shouldn't be difficult, given that we're talking about a man who looks like he's going to have an aortic aneurysm every time he remembers the existence of the *Guardian*.

So, let's talk vacations.

At their most basic, family holidays are all about the survival of the fittest. When Charles Darwin wrote his weighty tome *On the Origin of Species*, I'm sure he had the battle scars of many a fractious family holiday to the Galápagos Islands' Center Parcs in the back of his mind, shouting at his kids to start enjoying themselves given how much he'd paid for all this, and to stop throwing rocks at the turtles. Especially when he came up with the subtitle for his work, *Preservation of Favoured Races in the Struggle for Life*, he being paterfamilias and sire of ten children. Ten children, I know! To be fair, it's amazing that man got anything written in between all that siring.

Thankfully, I'm largely out the other end of family holidays now (give or take the odd trip I'm bribed to go on by Netflix) and can look back on them with the benefit of hindsight. I wish I'd known then what I know now, and hopefully by sharing some lessons I've learnt, you'll be able to keep your family from fracturing beyond repair.

As to my parents' input, I apologise in advance for anything that causes offence. Which may well be everything. Realistically, someone's going to be upset by something my father has written. Possibly Australians, probably the

French, almost definitely 'all women'. I also told my editor to keep a hawk-eye out for any prose opening with sentences like 'I'm not a racist, but ...' or 'I'll probably get in trouble for saying this ...' and to do a quick search for any retired colonial place names, but there's bound to be an errant 'Ceylon' that's slipped through the net or, heaven forbid, a stray 'dad joke'.

What I can assure you is that whatever they have to say has not just managed to weave past the publisher's legal department, but will also be a very different take on things to mine. It's certainly going to have colour. I'm already worrying about the reviews. Not necessarily from the critics; mainly from the Equality and Human Rights Commission. After you've read anything my father's written, pause, take a breath and say to yourself, 'It was a different time.'

As with all things, the most important lesson is to approach all family holidays with a degree of cynicism. The headline is simple: massively lower your expectations. If you go into them expecting a shitstorm, when it turns out to be simply a light shower – a small squall of turds – you will be pleasantly surprised, or at the very least have packed an umbrella.

And remember, as a teenager, even though you might think you're nearly out of the woods, you'll have to do it all again in twenty years' time with kids of your own! Or in a couple of years, depending on your use of contraception and your socio-economic background.

Preparation

THE MORE TIME IN BETWEEN family holidays, the longer one has to forget about the trials and tribulations of the last one. A bit like childbirth, as my mother is wont to remind me, usually in situations that are beyond embarrassing. I need not give specific examples: there is really no circumstance in which a son should ever be a party to that topic of conversation. No son has ever woken up in the morning and thought, 'You know what I'm in the mood for today? A spot of maternal vaginal banter.' It should go without saying that images of my mother in the stirrups are not ones on which I would wish to linger, or arrive at the first place, to be perfectly honest! Unfortunately, her propensity to talk about her 'strenuous labour' is matched only by my father's propensity to discuss my apparently 'equally strenuous' conception. Again, no time, place or universe exists in which that should ever be put into my, or indeed anybody else's, mind. And yet

I realise I've passed this on to you, basically perpetuating the cycle of abuse. Yet, possibly because every time they broach these topics of conversation I enter a kind of fugue state, even mental scars as deep as these can be healed with time. And it is time, the great healer, that can really come into its own when convincing a family that they might be ready again to load up the wheelie bags (Louis Vuitton), cancel the paper (*Telegraph*) and brave another trip into parts unknown (basically anywhere outside Putney).

Recollections of the blazing row you had with Mum and Dad over your role in encouraging your little sister to get her hair cornrowed by a Jamaican man on the beach (which, while an admirable attempt to engage with a different culture, did not go down well come autumn term at the Ladies' College) can fade as quickly as that year's tan. The memories of a tedious excursion to the Derwent Pencil Museum – a leaden experience in every sense of the word which at the time felt like it might push you to the brink of jamming a pair of the exhibits into your retinas, as your mother lined you up for a ten-minute photo shoot next to the world's biggest pencil – will soon be recalled in, dare I even say it, wistful reminiscence. It will all be looked back on with gratitude, or maybe just relief that the whole thing is over. I'm told kidnap victims feel similarly confusing feelings. In short, with time everything can fade. Other than tattoos. As anyone who's ever got spontaneous ink done on holiday knows, it will be with you for life. That and some STDs. But more on that later. The tattoos, not the STDs! This is about family holidays; don't worry, it doesn't get weird. Well, not in that way.

It always struck me as odd that people would be jealous

at school of the kids who went away on holiday with their families in the half-terms, as well as at Christmas, Easter and summer. This was seen as a luxury enjoyed only by the jet-setting few, whose parents could afford to whisk them off to the Maldives for ten days' scuba diving, while my half-term was stuck on an arts and crafts course in Richmond, run by a kaftan-clad cat lady with anger-management issues. Like an upper-middle-class version of Guantánamo Bay and just as guaranteed to break your spirit. But as I sat there, strapped to my potter's wheel, being told by Miss Mallard that men could never be trusted and the only being you could truly rely upon emotionally had four legs and licked itself clean, I never felt jealous for a minute of my even posher posh friends, swimming with the turtles. For as I'm sure Miss Mallard had thought to herself as she topped up her coffee mug with gin that day in yet another attempt to get through till lunch, it is possible to have too much of a good thing.

Trial Separation

The first piece of advice I would give you when preparing for a family holiday is this: it is of paramount importance to have a period of exile from your family in the lead-up to a holiday. The more extended this period can be, the better it will serve you. It will act as a much-needed palate cleanser from your nearest and dearest's foibles and follies. An emotional sorbet, if you will. Just a little circuit breaker, which could last anywhere between six and eight months. Just enough time to forget everything about them that annoys you. Maybe even a year.

This state of separation is obviously made considerably

easier if said 'nearest and dearest' have decided to pack you off each term to a boarding school hundreds of miles away. Your palate is so cleansed by the end of most terms, you've completely forgotten the taste altogether.

If you're not in the fortunate situation of living in a separate county to them for three-quarters of the year and have the cold, harsh reality of living under the same roof as your parents every day of the week, then finding a more creative solution is essential.

Maybe in the week before the family holiday you could book yourself into a nice hotel in London for a few nights – a little staycation before the vacation. It doesn't have to be the Ritz; somewhere modest like the Hilton or one of the minor Park Lane hotels will do just as well. I understand this option is more difficult if you're eight or nine and you lack the required disposable income to fork out on such a luxury (well done for picking this book instead of one by David Walliams – I hope I come out well in the book report). Still, at that age either you might want to start seriously thinking about saving up your pocket money for a little hotel fund because, trust me, it will only get more stressful once puberty takes a hold, or you should call a friend and arrange a sleepover for a few nights. Better still, pick a friend with a helicopter mum and a gorgon of a father to remind you that yours aren't that bad after all. I had a friend growing up whose dad was a hedge funder and liked clicking his fingers at waiters. One night in his company and I came back to Michael Whitehall like he was the Dalai Lama. More fitting than it might seem, since he was going through a phase of orange corduroy trousers at the time.

If such a stay is not possible due to diary restraints or a lack

of accommodating friends, your final option is to stage an argument with your parents (I could do this by saying I was thinking of getting a piercing or joining the Labour Party), lock yourself in your room for forty-eight hours under the guise of a hefty sulk and have a bit of 'you time'. They won't suspect a thing – most likely they'll imagine you're masturbating and leave you well alone.

If you're really lucky, you might be forgotten in your room and be left behind altogether, having to survive the next two weeks on your wits alone, a real-life *Home Alone*. For some children, the idea of being left behind by their parents is a nightmare; for me it was a fantasy. Many a stressful dash to the airport was spent daydreaming about my family being halfway to France and me being left to my own devices back in Putney, working out in my head how I was going to start rigging up the house, laying booby traps to defend myself in the event of a siege from comically clumsy burglars. Though quite why burglars would want to loot the Whitehall home is unclear, unless they were particularly keen on burgundy and books about David Niven. What a shock my mother and father would get when they returned from Provence to find Anne Stallybrass from number two, who they'd asked to come round and water the plants, lying prostrate on the front-door mat, having been knocked out cold by a makeshift trebuchet I'd fashioned out of a length of dressing-gown cord and one of my father's Winston Churchill Toby jugs.

I must stress that the purpose of this time apart from your family is all intended with the greatest will in the world: it is purely as a means of ensuring that when you're having breakfast, lunch and dinner with them every day for two weeks, your patience threshold is at its optimum capacity.

What we are dealing with is an endurance sport. You must view this training regime with the gimlet eye of an elite athlete and approach it with the discipline of an Olympic runner, a long-distance runner at that. After all, this is a marathon not a sprint.

Airing of Old Grievances

This is not to say that total separation from your family is advised in the run-up to the family holiday. Another vital piece of advice when preparing for your trip away is that you must at some point 'have it out' with them. Any underlying issues must be dealt with before the trip begins. Be under no illusions: whatever issues may be bubbling under the surface will, without fail, arise after a few complimentary glasses of prosecco and a five-hour flight! The disastrous job interview, the dodgy new boyfriend, the maxed-out over-draft, the fact that you still haven't passed your driving test: these landmines need to be trodden on before the holiday starts, for everyone's sake (only some of these are based on my own experiences – if I ever came home with a 'dodgy new boyfriend', I suspect Michael Whitehall and I would still be 'having it out' now). 'Having it out' may sound like a dreadful experience, but in the Whitehall household it's become such a regular feature of family life that we look for-ward to it, rather like Christmas. And by the way, it does also happen at Christmas. This doesn't mean that these issues won't be brought up again, repeatedly, on the holiday. The wounds will, of course, be reopened on numerous occasions, picked over forensically and discussed at length at every mealtime. But by having gone several rounds with them

already, you know their points of attack, how to parry the jabs. Hopefully, you will also have ascertained their points of weakness and developed tactics to shut down and kill the discussion in its tracks.

'Why does a boy of twenty-one not know how to drive?'

'Well, Daddy, because a boy of twenty-one cares about the environment more than a man of seventy and wants his grandchildren to know what a polar bear is.' (Beware: there is a danger here that your mother will hear the word 'grandchildren' and start opening her own separate line of attack; you do not want to be fighting on two fronts.)

'Don't you play that card with me, Jack.'

'Also, Daddy, if we all keep driving, then pretty soon we're all going to be underwater, which would be particularly problematic for you, as you can't swim. And on that note, why does a man of seventy not know how to swim?'

Long pause.

'Did I ever tell you about the time you were conceived?'

Some jabs are unparryable.

The 'No Friends' Policy

Although you might think that friends could be important allies on a family holiday, never, *ever* take one with you. Oh my, no! You think that this will be a good solution to the problem – a companion to retreat to when your family gets too much – but there is no greater test of a friendship than having them accompany you on your family holiday. I would love to see one friendship that survived it. Exposing a friend to the dark underbelly of your family and their inner workings and complicated dynamics is a sure-fire way to

unpick any bond you may have had. In my experience, a friend encountering your family dynamics is exactly like them seeing you naked. At best, they're going to pity you. At worst, they're going to tell other people about the scale of what they've witnessed.

There is nothing more mortifying than having your family's eccentricities laid bare by your holiday companion/survivor before all your classmates in the middle of a biology practical. It's impossible to focus on the important business of dissecting a pea when the class is hanging on every word of the maternal vaginal banter. So once a friend has seen beneath the bonnet, make sure you get them to either sign an NDA or just move school entirely. Harvey Chow, an overseas student from my prep school who accompanied me on a family trip to Mallorca one year, had his parents to thank for saving his life when they moved him back to Hong Kong. Had they not, I think I may have had to hire a hitman to ensure he kept quiet with regard to the morning he came down to the pool and found my mother sunbathing topless shrouded only partially by a well-thumbed copy of Alan Titchmarsh's autobiography, *Nobbut a Lad*. To this day, I don't know which element of the scene I find most problematic. To be honest, in the context of the holiday overall, it was probably a moment of light relief for Harvey, whose cultural background had already prompted the occasional remark from my father, and by 'occasional' I do mean on every occasion dinner appeared. I just know for sure that I am very thankful that Harvey now lives in a country on the other side of the world and, better still, one that bans social media. Long may that man remain censored by the state, for he knows – and has literally seen – too much!

The 'no friends' policy does, of course, later extend to partners too. But they will at some point have to experience your family, warts and all (believe me, there are warts aplenty), and if they can't handle this death by a thousand cuts and the stark and alarming reality of seeing what you will one day become, then perhaps it's best they take the opportunity to get out while they can. If anything, hurling them into the furnace is the most humane thing you can do, to see if they can handle the heat. If, by the third day, they're not by the side of the pool writing to Amnesty International for help, then they're probably a keeper.

A friend's role should be more like a Samaritan, someone on the other end of a phone, that you can confide in when it all gets too much. Synchronising with a friend or, thanks to the advent of WhatsApp, several friends, who are also on family holidays, is even better. Create a group and give it an appropriate name like 'Dispatches from the Hellmouth'. One can compare notes from the trenches and take solace from the fact that they are all having just as traumatic an experience as you are, in villas in every corner of the globe. What joy to see photos and videos of familial horrors, like your friend's 'cool' dad up on stage with the band in a hotel bar in Barbados, playing an impromptu and very much uninvited harmonica set. Or an Instagram story of your best mate's little sister on their camping holiday in Cornwall, necking a burly young lad from the caravan park called Pyramus. Hashtag: lol; hashtag: if the caravan's a-rocking . . . It quickly turns into a game of Embarrassing Families Top Trumps:

'My dad just did the waiter's accent while ordering, it was so awful.'

'Mine just tried to buy a gollywog at
an antiques fair.'

'OK, you win.'

Never Out of the Office

Working when on vacation can provide a welcome dis-traction and respite from endless discussions about which cousins are getting married and why Brexit will be a good thing for Britain in the end. The sort that have you binning the sunblock in the hope that a melanoma at least might provide you with a good excuse to leave early.

It's my strong belief that when on holiday with your family, the worst thing you can do is completely shut up shop, activate the out-of-office reply and put everything on the back burner. You have no idea of the comfortingly distracting qualities a normally tedious email from your accountant can be when you've just had a forty-five-minute discussion with your father about whether or not it is acceptable to call the fifty-year-old Spanish man cleaning your pool a 'pool boy'. Let alone whether or not it's offensive to comment, when said pool gentleman arrives five minutes later than expected, whether his 'donkey had a puncture'. Literally hours can be whiled away with your head buried deep in your laptop pretending to dissect a particularly complicated spreadsheet, when in reality you are looking at endless videos of cats being frightened by cucumbers. Who knew that was a thing? Seriously, if you haven't already, Google it now! Better yet, lucky you: keep that ace up your sleeve for the upcoming family holiday.

Another piece of advice that is often given to parents before their family holiday is to wear the children out before the journey, have them run around the garden and exhaust themselves or, as my mother used to do, get them to help clean the house. I don't know what had happened to the regular cleaner, but I know my mother's life has been made more and more difficult by modern anti-trafficking regulations. The theory is that a tired child is much easier company on a long car journey than one that is a coiled spring. I would venture that this can be a two-way street and that wearing out the parents can be just as important if you're going to get as far as South Mimms service station without hearing more than you're ever likely to want to about where Prince Harry 'went wrong'. I don't mean physically wear them out; the thought of trying to cajole my father into a few laps of the garden at any point during his life would have been a tricky proposition – he is no Captain Tom – but a certain degree of mental fatiguing is definitely both achievable and advisable.

Sourcing just the right news story on the TV is bound to set him off – find a bit of Owen Jones or maybe an interview with what my father likes to call 'a lady dressed up as a vicar' – and you might just be able to tease out a reaction and get a valuable rant out of his system. Draw the poison. Tory baiting, I call it. Get my father on to any of his pet hates – and there are enough to fill Battersea Dogs Home several times over – and you could provide power for a small- to medium-sized town with the energy expended ranting about them. You could use him as a substitute for wind turbines – which, come to think of it, are an excellent topic to start him going. It is, however, a high-risk strategy and you can easily overplay your hand. If you poke the hornets' nest too aggressively, you may end

up having to sit in a car from London to Devon listening to a five-hour lecture on why the Church of England has turned into a 'circus'; to be fair, that topic of conversation could keep him blabbering on to Devon, Connecticut.

Bringing some work to catch up on with you on holiday can be a great distraction, but when you literally bring your work with you, as in actual colleagues that you actually work with, it can backfire. I shall allow my father to extrapolate on this point with a long-winded anecdote about a family holiday he ruined by using it as a shameless networking opportunity. Get your *Who's Who 1997* at the ready – some extremely niche names are about to be dropped . . .

Michael: DON'T MIX BUSINESS WITH PLEASURE

My job as an actor's agent was a job of several parts. Firstly, I had to keep my clients happy and safe. For instance, I once took the blame for a prank that went horribly wrong when visiting Nigel Havers on a film set in Greece and he drove a hire car into the sea. It was a write-off and I, as the dutiful agent, paid the resulting bill, albeit a bill I was able to significantly negotiate down. Secondly, I had to permanently be on the hunt for new clients. One holiday in Barbados was spent being cheerfully and repeatedly thrashed at tennis by Sir Trevor McDonald, on the off chance that he might want a change of agent at some point and I would be cemented into his mind as a 'good sport'. He never called.

Most importantly of all, l had to make sure that my clients were always working and, to that end, network 24/7

and keep close to anyone in a position to give any of them a job. This sometimes blurred the lines between business and pleasure. I was prepared to do what I had to do to get my 10 per cent. Then, in the 1990s, Mrs Thatcher deregulated the television industry and this gave me the opportunity to get myself higher up the food chain by creating a production company with Nigel 'car-wrecker' Havers, whereby we could create work not just for him but ultimately for other clients as well. I now had a whole new set of people to cultivate: the programme commissioners.

1997 saw a large rump of my clients gainfully employed. Richard Griffiths was happily being the detective by day, chef by night in *Pie in the Sky* – God, it was a golden era of television. Dinsdale Landen was up north doing a Catherine Cookson, and Christopher Biggins? Well, he never stopped. Nigel Havers was starring in *Dangerfield* for the BBC, which meant, as he was busy, I could concentrate on producing a show for two other clients.

It was a show for a major channel and a plan was cooked up by the Head of Drama, as we were collaborating on the series, that it would be fun if we also went away on a family holiday together in Corfu. This was music to my ears, as it would provide me with major sucking-up opportunities and would also be a great change of pace for Mrs Whitehall, who would be able to enjoy supervising the childcare in a completely new location. Hilary secured an appropriate villa, which looked great in the holiday brochure, for the eight of us plus their Aussie au pair (I had my apprehensions about this, but reasoned that her nationality was arguably no fault of her own).

The initial problem that quickly became apparent on

arrival was that the villa, although very secluded and miles from the nearest town, was unfortunately not miles from the local pig farm. Although the pigs were fenced off, with less than adequate wire fencing, the noise and smell of them was not. There was quite a lot of noise and smell; these animals were literally 'as happy as pigs in shit'.

The first task was to allocate the rooms. Thinking it politic to defer to the TV executive, we ended up drawing the short straw and being assigned a room with a tiny double bed (called a queen size, I believe, though one can't quite imagine Her Majesty being so disposed to enforced snuggling) and no external windows; its sole window opened on to a corridor, with a sofa positioned below it on which the head honcho, a chain smoker, had taken up residence to enjoy his first of many cigarettes, billowing clouds of smoke into our bedroom.

As ever on so many of our family holidays, I had calls to catch up on; the entertainment business, being a 24/7 industry, is no respecter of evenings, weekends or holidays. Many, many family Sunday lunches have been ruined by an actor calling at 1 p.m. to discuss a one-man show he was thinking of doing at the Edinburgh Festival the following summer, or some urgent brouhaha that had to be resolved on the set of *Lovejoy*. Worst of all was a pre-internet/mobile phone trip to Barbados where I spent the majority of the holiday in the office of the hotel we were staying in, leaving a pregnant Hilary in sole charge of a three- and a two-year-old, commandeering their phone in order to try and unravel the chaos left by one of my actors having been sacked from a new BBC crime series after the first week of filming, as the director had decided he had made a terrible mistake in casting him.

I digress. Now firmly in the mobile phone era, the only place I could get a phone signal was in the middle of the villa tennis court. Unfortunately, it turned out that the TV head's wife was an obsessive tennis player and wanted to teach her unwilling daughter, Saffron, how to play, thereby spending most of the holiday occupying the court. She was none too keen on my endlessly wandering along the net waving my Nokia brick around like some sort of superannuated line judge. Making phone calls became a nightmare, unless they were made very early in the morning or after dark. As it turned out, this was somewhat of a blessing, as for most of the day it was as hot as Hades out there. Hardly a wonder that the peoples of the Mediterranean have achieved so little in the last two millennia; they must have spent most of the time looking for shade. When the mother–daughter combo was on the court, I was rendered unreachable. In an emergency, I might have been able to clamber into the umpire's chair, even if it may have slightly defeated the whole object of the holiday in the first place: given that its purpose was to suck up to this family, it probably wasn't wise to distract the daughter from her tennis lesson by subjecting her to an hour-long discussion with Nigel Havers about whether he was too old to play Jack Worthing in *The Importance of Being Earnest* (for what it's worth, my opinion was that Nigel has class, and class is ageless).

The TV executive himself had decided that Saffron should also learn to swim, clearly intent on cultivating some sort of renaissance woman, so when she wasn't on the tennis court with her mother, she was in the pool with her father, trying – with minimal success – to overcome her fear of water. This made the pool a no-go area for our three children, who by

then were all excellent swimmers, thanks to Hilary (talents I believe she largely cultivated in an attempt to taunt me), and wanted to hurl themselves (usually naked) both in and out of the pool with reckless abandon. Another problem at the poolside was that it abutted the inadequate wire fence of the pig unit. This was no barrier to the millions of flies, swarming over not just the pool area but across the entire property. It's a wonder we didn't all come down with swine flu.

As with most family holidays, especially ones shared with other families, there were many flashpoints, particularly when dealing with their recalcitrant au pair. She was far from the clichéd Aussie willing pair of hands. Had she been at Gallipoli, she would only have been an asset to the Turks. Everything was too much trouble for her and she spent most of her time either lying on her bed or lying by the pool. Which, given her employers' extensive and time-consuming sporting programme for their daughter, didn't seem to bother them. The apotheosis to this state of affairs came as we hit the midpoint of the holiday, after she cut her foot walking across the drive with no shoes on. A trip to the local hospital and several stitches later she was good to go. Well, actually not good to go, as she couldn't walk properly and certainly couldn't venture into the pool. Hilary, being a saint, made her a cup of coffee the following morning and took it to her in her room, which incidentally had a lovely window opening on to the garden, which was more than ours did. Moments later, as Hilary was in the kitchen loading the dishwasher, the au pair hobbled past, dressed in a sarong and clutching a fashion magazine.

'Oh, by the way, Hilary,' she said, 'for future reference, I take two sugars in my coffee.' Not even so much as a 'G'day'.

We just about got through the remaining weeks, circum-navigating further flashpoints by drinking at lunchtime – and most other times, come to think of it. Alcohol can be a panacea for many holiday ills – nature's anaesthetic. Most of the flashpoints were caused by my children, for instance their inability to cut Saffron, a serial sore loser, some slack when it came to winning. It reminded me of a weekend in Dorset staying with an even more important channel controller when I had to reprimand Jack for repeatedly and unedifyingly fist-pumping the air as he romped further ahead and almost out of sight in a game of croquet with our host, who was equally competitive and took a very dim view of being thrashed by a thirteen-year-old on his own sumptuous back lawn. At one point, as Jack cavorted around him issuing a stream of high-pitched sledging, I thought this gentleman was going to put the mallet to a use for which it was not competitively intended.

But back to Corfu and we continued to have problems curbing our children's competitive spirit. This wasn't the only excess that we had difficulty curbing: Mrs TV Executive was definitely not a fan of my children's aforementioned proclivity for nudity. And despite her constant nagging of Jack in particular to 'quieten down and put some bloody clothes on', she never got his volume level much below a nine and rarely persuaded him into clothes, except at mealtimes, when she absolutely insisted on it. And the ever-present cigarette smoke could have brought our holiday to a premature end had it not been for Hilary talking me down on an hourly basis, especially first thing in the morning as it permeated our bedroom. Salmon have been smoked less thoroughly than we were that week. No, Hilary and I were

charming and smarmy in equal measure at all times, right up until we kissed his tobacco-stained cheeks goodbye as we left Heathrow for home. It had nearly killed me, as being obsequious and accommodating is a long distance away from my natural demeanour, but it's amazing what you can find yourself capable of when money is involved.

The final irony of all this was that a couple of weeks after we got home, the drama controller called me to say that he had been offered a move to factual that would take him away from the creative side of things; although, like so many senior TV drama execs, his proximity to them in the first place had been more theoretical than real. So all that effort had been in vain. Three weeks on a Greek pig farm with their hot-housed child, nursing their lame au pair and the early stages of lung cancer from all that second-hand smoke and I didn't even get a second series!

Well, I think we can all agree, that's a cautionary tale in why you should never pimp out your family to try to get a television series commissioned. I have no idea how that lesson is in any way transferable to your lives, but you have been warned that large swathes of this book could possibly be accused of being a touch 'unrelatable'. I'd hoped Michael might have been able to open his account with something a little more accessible than the story about the time he got cock-teased by a drama controller. Still, stick with us as the next bit's very relatable: it's all about preparing the house before departing. You know, stuff that all families do: setting alarms, cancelling papers, giving the butler a week's leave.

Practicalities and Security

There are, of course, practical preparations for a holiday that mustn't be overlooked. Plants must be watered, newspapers cancelled, neighbours must be informed of your movements and a running-away bag must be packed and left in your room for a speedy departure when you get back in case it's gone really tits up.

Preparations for your return are just as important as preparations for your departure. As my dad would always sing in his worst Frank Sinatra impression, always getting the lyrics slight wrong, 'It's fun to go travelling, but it's so much better to come home.'

I would add to that lyric: 'It's fun to go travelling, but it's so much better to come home, provided you have remembered to turn down the central heating thermostat.' Especially in our house, where my father likes to have the temperature set to a level usually found only in old people's homes or tropical greenhouses. At night you can see steam creeping out across the doormat. I'm sure the neighbours think he's growing weed. If you forget to turn it right down, you come back to a Turkish hammam, all the candles melted and the living room looking like a Salvador Dalí. You should never have to return from a holiday to a hotter climate than the one you've just left.

Another pre-departure headache is security, which ascends to eye-watering levels of importance. It is my mother's self-appointed prerogative – and some might say obsession – to make sure that everything is hidden from the sight of eagle-eyed thieves, even items that they would have no interest in taking. For example, the single tennis shoe

that's been left on the front porch for months, which results in a last-minute dash back from the car to hide it behind a flower pot lest it tempt any light-fingered, one-legged, racket-sport enthusiast that might be hopping by.

Everything must be locked, double-locked, checked, then checked again and, in most cases, driven back to to be checked for a third time. I don't know what criminal masterminds she thinks are operating on the streets of Putney, plotting to break through her defences. I haven't seen Ocean's Eleven hanging around. Not that all this will put her mind at rest; there will still be a moment of blind panic at Heathrow when Mother has a minor mental breakdown in the queue for Pret a Manger because she realises that she didn't padlock the bread bin. We have to prise her clenched fingers off a can of sparkling Yoga Bunny before she calms down.

The list of security measures she must undertake before departure is overwhelming – things like tightening all the window locks to the point where my father will have to get a builder in when we return. That's assuming my mother can remember the 'extra safe place' where she has stashed the key. To be honest, instead of a builder, they'd be better off bringing in an occupational therapist. The levels of panic induced by the thought that she may have left the shed door ajar are such that she is unable ever to truly relax by the pool reading a magazine (perhaps explaining why she ends up using Alan Titchmarsh books as clothing rather than reading matter), so haunted is she by the fear that she may have unleashed a hoard of lawnmower thieves back home running amok through her shed ripping open boxes of lawn feed and scattering Unwins seed packets around in an orgy of incredibly mild devastation. No comfort is found by pointing

out to her that any criminal would have to either be craned or winched over the house into the garden or make his (or her) way by crawling undetected, commando-style, through at least eight of our neighbours' gardens, scaling the fences in between, to gain access to said unsecured shed in what seems like an unnecessary amount of *Bravo Two Zero*-style effort in order to steal a pair of rusty pruning shears. No, the entire start to the holiday is spent on edge, with these wicked fears hanging over her like the secateurs of Damocles, until she finally breaks and telephones to ask the neighbours' son to vault the garden fence, confirm that the shed is indeed bolted shut and that the lawnmower is safely inside, with the wheel clamp she attached to it untampered with.

Michael: SECURITY LIGHTS

Now, I love my wife dearly but by far the worst detail of the pre-holiday to-do list, one that has repeatedly tested our marriage to the limit and that I dread above all others, is the installation of the automated light timers. Clearly, in order to retain his own sanity, Jack has wiped this particular obsession from his mind. But Hilary can spend literally a whole day setting up these wretched little devices. And do you know what the worst aspect of this particular and – I'm going to be kind here – neurotic problem is? She insists on doing it several days before departure for two inexplicable reasons.

I will grudgingly admit, as I do very little towards the pre-departure preparations (and 'very little' is probably overestimating my contribution), that the first justification for this is just about acceptable.

'I will be too busy with packing and several other last-minute preparations on the day of departure.' Packing on the day of departure? Is she joking? As Jack will no doubt reveal elsewhere, his mother takes packing to a whole other level of lunacy.

But her second reason is just baffling.

'I think it's important that any burglar who is watching the house and noting the pattern of lights going on and off randomly will be observing them for a few days, hopefully including these few days when we are still in residence and going in and out of the house. They will therefore assume that is the pattern that occurs when we are at home. Therefore, it follows that when we are away, they will see the pattern of lights and assume that we are still at home. Clever, eh?'

No, my darling wife, it's insane.

This takes overthinking and over-complicating to new extremes. Does she really think that any opportunistic burglar worth his salt has got evenings to spare watching the ridiculous pageant of lights going on and off randomly in our boringly suburban house, like a dazzling spectacle from the Pyramid Stage, a sort of muted version of The Rolling Stones at Glastonbury? And if they are operating this system of round-the-clock surveillance, they're probably going to take less notice of the change in the lights and afford more importance to the moment when we all emerge from the house carrying suitcases.

What this does mean is that we are all given very clear instructions not to tamper with any of the devices and certainly, under no circumstances, are we ever to turn a light on or off manually, as she wouldn't have time to re-programme

them. As a result, in the days leading up to every holiday, I will either be plunged into darkness mid-chapter when trying to finish Volume 1 of Charles Moore's excellent biography of Margaret Thatcher, so that I only need trouble myself with taking Volumes 2 and 3 on holiday, thereby avoiding incurring excess weight charges (I realise I'm going into a lot of detail here, but I know you the reader will want a rounded picture of the man you will already have identified as the hero of this story) or be woken up at 5 a.m. by the bedroom lights suddenly bursting into life and giving us both barrels of their unforgiving 100 watts. There are enough things that interrupt the slumber of a gentleman of a certain age without his own bedroom doing an impression of someone tripping the searchlights on a breakout from Stalag Luft.

On one memorable occasion on the eve of a family holiday, this obsession came back to bite her in a costly way, both financially and emotionally. I was tucked up in bed, happily reading a detailed volume of Churchill's *The Great War* (always a favourite – I enjoy a story with a happy ending), when I was plunged into darkness by one of Hilary's wretched devices. I struggled out of bed, forgetting that I had removed my glasses and put them beside me so that I could have a closer inspection of some detailed footnotes on the Battle of the Somme. My eyesight is not great, so my glasses are not merely an essential, ever-present companion, they also have every available visual aid: varifocal, anti-glare, scratch-resistance, extra-thin lenses, and that's before you even get to the frames. As I stumbled towards the light switch, I knocked something off the bed, and the crunch of broken glass under my bare

foot told me that I had broken my glasses beyond repair. In an attempt to remove my foot from the scene, I stubbed several of my toes on the divan. I know I'm painting a heart-rending picture for you, the reader. As a wordsmith, it's one of the talents I share with Dickens. My entire dictionary of shouted expletives brought Hilary haring up several flights of stairs, waking up all three children and the dog. She would probably insist in her defence that, even if in a roundabout way, her method worked: my swearing and yelling would indeed have deterred any local burglars watching from the bushes and steered them clear of the madhouse in front of them. They would probably decide they were better off targeting our neighbour, Anne Stallybrass – always a soft touch.

This very small moment on the eve-of-holiday departure not only cost a small fortune to replace the glasses but also meant that I had to travel for two weeks in my considerably less loved spare pair. In addition, and to my mind 100 per cent as a result of the extreme trauma to my foot, a particularly virulent bout of gout accompanied me for most of our trip away.

The next step in pre-departure preparation is for all newspaper deliveries and magazine subscriptions to be cancelled; in the case of the literature that my parents subscribe to, preferably for ever. All the magazines my mother reads have images of kitchens on the front; all the ones my father reads have cartoons of Boris Johnson dancing on a European flag and headlines like 'His hour of triumph' – the kind of magazine where a year's subscription comes with a free case of port, which you wouldn't think was a very good business

model, given that most of the readers are already drinking themselves to death, and it's a toss-up which gets them first, cirrhosis of the liver or apoplectic shock at the very existence of vegan mayonnaise. But these cancellations have to be made. No one wants to return to their home to find their front door has literally been walled in by copies of the *Daily Mail*, my father having to call the local newsagents and give him an earful.

'We've travelled all the way from Turkey and we can't get in.'

'Daddy, it's what the *Daily Mail* would have wanted.'

'Shut up, Jack!'

Furthermore, the pantry and fridge must be stocked with home comforts for your return. After a long week of trying to convince yourself you like pastry and sliced cheese for breakfast, there is nothing better than returning to the dark treacly embrace of Marmite. For me, the best of all return meals, though, is a steaming plate of baked beans on toast. The restorative qualities of that meal; a plate of flatulence-inducing, childhood joy. A meal that laughs in the face of your five-a-day. A dish that reminds you that even if your parents drive you to the point of madness, they still know what is best for you; a rare dinner that even my father could whip up, if he was sober enough to open the tin. Or knew where in the house the kitchen even was. And though you would never refer to another nation's cuisine with the same terminology as your old man (certainly not while you still want to have a career), buried beneath his light topsoil of xenophobia grows a home truth that 'no amount of foreign muck will ever beat good old British beans on toast'. As you bask in that fluorescent glow of the ultimate comfort food,

you don't even feel the need to point out to him that Heinz is an American company founded by the son of German immigrants.

Finally, one footnote – and this is the gravest piece of advice that I will share with you. It is so important that if you were to disregard everything else I have told you in this chapter just to make room for this one precious nugget, it would not be in vain. If you want to avoid having to remortgage your house and don't want to see you and your family financially ruined, living on the street penniless and destitute, make sure you turn off your data roaming. Even in Europe, thanks to Daddy.

Packing and Passports

THE NEXT STAGE IN your departure preparation is working out what you are actually going to take with you: which hat, what book, how many children. There will be much discussion about what items are deemed 'essential'; can a shoe tree really be classified as that? Surely that's a luxury item, not an 'essential'? I doubt it's on the Navy SEAL equipment list. Over-packers and under-packers may disagree on much; phrases like 'oh we can just get that at the airport' will be bandied about. There remain, however, some non-negotiables that you're going nowhere without. First and foremost, a passport.

Lost Passports

Hell hath no fury like a father whose child lost its passport, especially when this overwhelmingly important

fact does not come to light until they are standing at the BA check-in desk. (It goes without saying that this really is the be-all and end-all of packing. At the bare minimum, a passport and the clothes on your back will suffice, as many people in the latter stages of their gap years have triumphantly found.) I have never felt a fear like the fear I experienced having to tell my father that I couldn't find my passport at the airport on the return leg of one trip. I don't think I've ever seen him react like that, with the possible exception of the first time he heard a woman speak on *Test Match Special*. Watching the vein start twitching on his forehead, his fists whiten, clenched to the point of constricting the blood vessels in his hands, as his face began to turn that same deep crimson of the passport that I'd misplaced (this was back in the long-forgotten days when the colour of your passport was unremarkable, rather than the single most important thing that has ever mattered to anyone, ever). I'm first accused of being 'simple' in front of an embarrassed check-in lady, and then again at the information desk, as the first call is put in to the British Consulate to make plans for how we are going to navigate this diplomatic clusterfuck and get me back home passportless. I think he'd quite happily have left me there for the rest of my life like the bloke in *The Terminal*. I've never seen a man angrier.

I've also never seen a man backtrack less elegantly when, retrieving some more of this country's 'Monopoly money' to pay for the 'mucked-about-with lunch' in the 'ghastly' airport café, the offending passport was discovered to have been in his briefcase all along, hidden between a copy of the *Spectator* and the fourteen-page holiday itinerary my mother had helpfully printed out.

I've now lost my passport so many times that I think, in the future, I might just staple it to my arm. It's probably the only piercing my father would actually approve of. But let's put the passport to one side for a second, remembering of course where we put it.

Packing Etiquette

Packing for holiday is an exercise taken to military proportions for some people; not for them chucking a toothbrush and a spare pair of pants into a backpack and heading off into the wide blue yonder. No, they require weeks of preparation, Excel spreadsheets and detailed research on the places that they are visiting. If they didn't need a holiday before the planning started, they definitely did by the end. My dear saintly mother is an assiduous proponent of this method. Packing brings out her latent OCD and threatens her thirty-three-year marriage to my father on an annual basis, as she ramps up to a minimum of DEFCON 3 in her bid to be ready for whatever the holiday has to throw at her. Churchill made fewer plans for going to Normandy than she does for a two-week trip. As my mother would say, 'We shall fight them on the beaches, in whatever terrain, weather or dress code is required.'

Historically, this is how the whole thing used to play out. The process started weeks before the departure date. It was at this point that several items of my clothing went missing. Could this be the work of those famously time-rich burglars of south-west London? No – because they would soon reappear in neat piles on the spare room bed. Colour coordinated, and stacked in size order with Post-it notes on the

top, indicating which pile belonged to which child. This was necessary from an early age, as I always enjoyed 'borrowing' my sister Molly's clothes, particularly from her fancy dress costumes, as they were generally far more interesting than my own and, more importantly, it was a quick and easy way to wind up my father. One feather boa has much the same effect as waking him up from an afternoon nap with a chorus of 'Oh, Jeremy Corbyn'. He only has himself to blame: you bring up a young boy on a diet of seeing your client Christopher Biggins in pantomime each year, he's not going to fear donning a frock from time to time for a cheap laugh. Be that as it may, my sister's and my shared '*Pocahontas* phase' was a particularly dark period in the Whitehall family dressing-up chronicles for Daddy. To be fair, as I always said to him, he should have just joined in – with his accent and his attitude to race relations, he could easily have passed as one of the baddies.

During the weeks running up to the holiday, whatever the dressing-up phase was, the exchange with my mother was invariably the same, something along the lines of: 'Jack, please go and take off that *Power Rangers* costume and put on something more sensible. But do not, I repeat, do not take anything from the spare bed.' You couldn't take anything without her knowing – I think she must have had a trick with the Post-it notes – maybe she aligned it with the angle of the pouch on my Y-fronts so she could tell if it had been disturbed, like something out of *Tinker Tailor Soldier Spy*. 'And don't think that costume's coming with us. I'm not spending my holiday calming your father down when you try to go sightseeing in a pink leotard and helmet. It's my holiday too, remember.'

Poor Kimberly, she never did get to see the Arc de Triomphe.

When it comes to packing, some people just have a gift, a God-given ability to pack with poise, patience and precision. My mother, for example, can tetrisise a suitcase with a tactical skill that defies the laws of physics. She can make a Smythson travel bag seem like Doctor Who's TARDIS. It's like she's using an estate model of Mary Poppins' handbag. She has tricks that only mothers seem to know about. They must share them with each other on the deepest darkest reaches of Mumsnet or in the comments section of the *Daily Mail* under articles about Kate Middleton. All the fat shaming and pseudoscience is just to put the rest of us off the scent. My mind was blown the first time she showed me you could put socks inside the cavity of your shoes to maximise suitcase space and that clothing could be rolled rather than folded. I was Luke Skywalker; she was my luggage Yoda. I can just imagine her with a pile of jumpers in one hand and an incredibly small carry case in the other, saying, 'No! Try not! Pack, or pack not. There is no "'try".' She can also dismantle any household appliance, no matter how unwieldy, and get it into a suitcase. You'll marvel at her gliding effortlessly through customs with a tiny wheelie bag trailing behind her, and think, 'How the hell has she managed to fit a Dyson hairdryer, two fans and an entire Corby trouser press into that?' She'd be great at disposing of a body – fortunately not something we've had to do on a holiday . . . yet. I reckon, with the right equipment, she could get a grown man into a trunk in about twenty minutes. If the cartels are hiring, look no further. She'd probably be a pretty good mule too. She'd have swallowed eight condoms full of cocaine, and still be like, 'Hang on, if I bunch them up in my small intestine,

I'm sure there's room for another.' And by God the amount of contraband she'd be able to vacuum-pack into one of her John Lewis packing cubes!

I am a different beast. I have always packed with the haste of an adulterer who's heard the crunch of a husband's footsteps on the gravel drive. As a child, it was a couple of football shirts, the Game Boy and a change of pants (optional); half do up the broken zip on my *Thunderbirds* backpack and I'm hot to trot. As an adult, it's a pretty similar situation, except the Game Boy is now an iPad, the football shirts are Thomas Pink linens and I finally fixed the zip on my *Thunderbirds* backpack. Also – always a change of pants now. Once bitten, twice shy.

My father, on the other hand, packs like a nineteenth-century viceroy heading off to the Raj for a couple of years. I will allow him to go into more detail in a section that reads a bit like an edition of *GQ* that's been guest-edited by Edward VII.

Michael: HOLIDAY WARDROBE

My holiday wardrobe has evolved over the years, in large part due to the changing fashions, the intervention of my wife and latterly the embarrassment and attendant mockery of my children. My early holidays with Hilary and subsequently the children did not benefit from taking place during the late 1980s and '90s, eras not especially remembered for their high fashion, save for Mrs Thatcher, who was always impeccably turned out. These decades are remembered mostly for some fashion frights. Enormous shoulder pads

were de rigueur, as were pixie boots, leg warmers, lace, pearls, polka dots and either mullets or perms, which allegedly offered extra body to one's locks. And the women didn't fare much better.

I managed to swerve most of these horrors, although I must confess there are a couple of photographs in existence of me sporting not only a perm but also double denim. The excuse for this would be the same as the one I offer for so many things, namely that I was probably drunk. In my office, a blue pinstripe suit, white shirt and restrained silk tie were my daily garb. When I was in a jaunty mood, a trilby hat might have been added to the look and occasionally I would go rogue and wear a bow tie. I like to think of the overall effect as a sort of 'streetwise Henry Blofeld'.

Holidays were a whole different story and far trickier to navigate. Hilary talked me into embracing the idea that although I didn't actually play any sport (I was the 1st XI Scorer and 1st XV Orangeman at Ampleforth), I should at least consider the notion of sportswear. However, my definition of what that constituted differed considerably from the norm; I was just about content to don a polo shirt, for instance, before you get the image of me strolling down the Promenade des Anglais in a 'shell suit'.

Our first holiday together was a location visit to Greece to see a young Nigel Havers, an even younger Hugh Grant and the perennially old Julian, now Lord, Fellowes, who, like a very fine Margaux, has matured beautifully with age. Sadly, the film in question, *Lord Elgin and Some Stones of No Value*, has not. Although the temperature in the Peloponnese where they were filming seldom dropped much below thirty degrees Celsius, Julian's dress code, when he was not

wearing the clerical outfit that was his costume as the Revd Philip Hunt, was strictly long trousers and a long-sleeved shirt. If only I had followed suit, but I was still in the business of trying to impress my new young fiancée (although one would have thought my personality contained enough of what young people these days call the 'wow factor' not to require any additional sartorial effort), who even at this early stage had taken charge of my holiday wardrobe, with catastrophic results. Some of the items worn on that first holiday were staples I persevered with for far, far too long; in particular, shorts. Some men are not built for the abbreviated trouser. An early example of my own struggle with shorts was on honeymoon and, to be brutally honest, this should have been the apotheosis of my relationship with them. For some inexplicable reason, I selected a pair of shorts that were so short, that I'm amazed they were able to contain or conceal anything. Though as it was our honeymoon, this was frankly less of an issue, as the hectic bedroom schedule was assisted by as few raiment obstructions as possible. I coordinated said shorts with a pair of soft, calf-leather, flat, lace-up Pineapple dance shoes. Don't ask. All I can say in my defence is this was the eighties. The entire outfit was topped off by a pair of oversized glasses, the whole ensemble in bright turquoise. I looked like a Christopher Biggins tribute act.

Despite this, I persevered in my pursuit of the perfect shorts. A further incarnation, decades later, was the very long short, unveiled in St Tropez. I was, by then, relying on my children to critique my sartorial misdemeanours. I am still not sure how these shorts managed to get through their exacting fashion metric (which seemed rather more stringent upon me than on their own excursions into Native American

transvestism), but they did. As did the three-quarter-length, unstructured, linen short, that made it into the suitcase that year. It was broadly felt by all concerned that in relation to the display of my calves and ankles, less was more. A family intervention was staged and upon arrival back in London they were, I am glad to say, banished to a charity shop in Barnes, and hopefully bought by a man a foot shorter than me and repurposed as full-length trousers.

I suppose I should also deal with the thorny question of swimwear. As Jack will tell anyone at any given opportunity, I try not to indulge in any water-based activity unless I absolutely have to. Hilary once made the mistake of leaving me and my friend Martin Jarvis in charge of our three small children in the swimming pool of a holiday villa. It was as she was struggling to make herself understood at the fish counter in the local supermarket that she had the sickening realisation that she had forgotten that neither of us could swim and that if any of the children happened to stray into the deep end, they would probably end up lying at the bottom of the pool. It was a miracle that she was not stopped by the local police on her breakneck drive back to the villa, minus the fish for supper. None of the children drowned, but we did go hungry, so something of a mixed outcome.

The holiday shoe is a mystery to me. My sadly departed but much missed father-in-law was a lover of the open-toe sandal paired with a sock – as great a fashion faux pas as it is possible to make. I suppose that logically it is not dissimilar to wearing a peephole bra over a cardigan. Another disaster on the shoe front is trainers on the over sixties. Even Paul McCartney can't pull them off – and someone should really tell him he can't – so what hope does a mere mortal like me

have? It's impossible for a gentleman of a certain age to wear trainers without looking as though they've been prescribed by a podiatrist. I don't care how comfortable they are, it is not becoming for a senior citizen to select this option in the footwear department; they are called 'trainers' for a reason, and given that the only training I do is taking the dog for a walk or occasionally ironing a shirt, perhaps the odd crossword to keep the mind alive, why on earth would I require footwear that has been designed for elite athletes? I might as well go about wearing a gum shield and a cricket box. It's as preposterous as the sight of a grown man in a football shirt – who are they kidding? And don't even start me on the slider or its even uglier and unfathomable cousin the flip-flop! I have never understood how anyone can get their foot into a flip-flop, let alone keep it on their foot while walking. In Australia, when filming *Travels with my Father*, I discovered that they refer to them as 'thongs', although no one thought to pass this information on to me before we got there. You can imagine my concern when an eager young production runner called Steve bounded over to me at breakfast one morning and asked if I'd packed my thongs for the beach scene.

'I most certainly have not!' I replied, affronted at such a thought. When he suggested I might borrow a pair of his, as we looked about the same size, I nearly spat out my tea! I wasn't sure whether this was impertinence or an attempt at flirtation. Either way, I was about to report it to our producer when Jack came down and set me straight on this unfortunate case of 'lost in translation'. I wonder what on earth they call the other thong? Still, you won't see me dead in either type!

I eventually concluded that I should just be my own man on the holiday wardrobe front. So, my default position for the last fifteen years or so has been to pack at least two suits. Pale, lightweight suits for warmer and tropical backdrops; smart, dark suits for cooler climes and any unexpected funerals. Although, if I'm honest, I like to cover all eventualities, so will often travel with two of each, thereby making temperature regulation easier. I also like to have the back-up of some casual attire: a couple of sports jackets and some flannel and summer trousers. All of these can be worn with lightweight, white shirts, with or without a tie (ideally with), of which I always include an assortment of plain and patterned. These I colour-match with a selection of handkerchiefs and socks. The look is finished off with a pair of Church's brogues, a selection of soft, French, suede lace-ups in different colours and, for very casual moments, some leather slip-ons. With a few belt options, I am good to go. As you can see, the key is to travel light and be as versatile as possible.

Needless to say, as in almost everything in life apart from cooking, badminton and Scrabble, my wife's packing skills are far superior to mine. So, when I say I like to pack, it does of course fall to her to do the packing for both of us. She enjoys doing it, and who am I to meddle in her simple pleasures? And I should add that her gifts are not confined to just packing. Having a younger wife is particularly advantageous in coping with the manoeuvring of luggage and other travel items, let alone the various other perks that I am happy to go into detail about elsewhere in the book.

One final item has been added to this ever-growing list of essentials as a direct result of our trip to Vietnam, where

the bathroom facilities at the beach hut we were staying in rather harrowingly included a very sorry-looking bucket and 'sluice' in the corner for post-lavatorial ablutions. I had to assume all more substantial toileting arrangements had been destroyed during the long conflict with America. 'Sluicing' for me falls into the same category as electric shaving or watching Channel 4: I've got this far avoiding it, why start now? I have subsequently added toilet paper to my list of essentials to avoid any such indignities in the future. It is a precaution for which I am mercilessly mocked by my son, partly as it is him that has to carry around the briefcase full of said toilet roll (in all honesty, a small recompense for the astronomical price of his supposed education) and partly because my not engaging in the custom of sluicing is seen as some sort of affront to their culture. He can get as woke as he likes on me; every man has his limits and this, it turns out, is mine. I'm willing to bow and take off my hat in a temple, but I am not washing my arse with a wooden spoon! If that makes me 'culturally insensitive' then it is a cross I shall have to bear. As far as I'm concerned, Jack can mock me all he likes; I take solace in the fact that deep down I know he's far more pampered than he lets on to the camera when we make these shows. He won't be smirking when he's squatting over a bucket sluicing away after he's been unable to crack the code on my briefcase brimming with soft, pillowy Andrex. Sorry, son, but as they say: you win some, you sluice some.

To be honest, if I was that desperate, I'd just steal one of those polka-dot pocket squares he was banging on about. As you recover from the image of my father in shorts or indeed

the idea of his 'post-lavatorial ablutions' which is literally the poshest way anyone has ever referred to cleaning their arse, I shall move on to the very serious and contentious issue of organised fun.

Bored Games and Board Games

Packing as many distractions for a family holiday as you can is a good idea: anything that can dispel the boredom or – even worse – the conversation. iPads, laptops and gaming consoles can be very useful for switching off, but under no circumstances should you take cards or board games. These are merely potential flashpoints masquerading as fun. The most innocuous of games can end up with threats to disinherit, for when played with your family, even Hungry Hippos can descend into the Red Wedding from *Game of Thrones*. All games must be approached with the same caution with which you would approach an actual hippopotamus.

Take Scrabble, the most civilised pastime going, an intellectual frolic of words and letters. Like *Countdown* but without the bits with numbers that only weirdos can actually do. It's testament to how vicious it can get that I say I would rather play Strip Twister with my family than Scrabble.

At this point, my mother wants to tell a story about her and my father's honeymoon, which she assures me is Scrabble-related. The thoughts of their honeymoon is something that inspires not so much a sinking feeling as an upchucking one. I have not read it for fear of what sordid details of their extracurricular activities on that trip I might be exposed to . . .

Hilary: **SCRABBLEGATE**

Scrabble has got form in our family history, as it nearly caused the end of my marriage, virtually before it had begun. I have to take ownership of this story and I should preface it by admitting that it was not one of my finest hours.

Scrabble has proved to be a contentious inclusion in the family games panoply, which, to be honest, was always pretty limited. One thing Michael and I discovered early on in our relationship was the fact that board games were not our 'go to' form of indoor entertainment. Nowadays we spend our evenings playing games that all couples of our age will be familiar with, games like hide-and-seek, which we tend to play with Michael's mobile phone; 'Fish or chicken for dinner?', where I ask my husband that question over and over again, and 'Why did I come in here?', a game where I try to guess why Michael came into the room when he's forgotten. But we have arrived at this routine having given more conventional forms of entertainment a bloody good go. Unfortunately, chess, draughts and Trivial Pursuit left us cold, while Risk and Battleship reminded Michael too much of his youth. Scrabble, however, as far as Michael was concerned, was the only game worth playing. He *loved* it!

The first time it caused havoc in our lives was on our honeymoon, a three-island trip to the Seychelles. It was the trip of a lifetime and I had done my usual months of research as to when was the optimum time to embark on this adventure, picking a time when, according to several travel agents, we were 'guaranteed sunshine'.

As I stepped off the plane, I mentioned to Michael how

green and verdant it was for a tropical island, and it wasn't long before we found out why. On the interminable bus transfer from the airport it started to rain, and as one, as if they had been choreographed, all the locals put up their umbrellas, which I had initially and quite mistakenly believed to be beach parasols. These, on some occasions quite heavy rain showers, were a daily occurrence during our three-week stay; it was either boiling hot or raining, offering us a Hobson's choice of conditions. This was fine during our first of the island stays in Mahé, the main island of the archipelago, as it had plenty of things to do and places to visit. We had also been given an enormous hotel room, in which we were able to employ the services of my ever-present travelling companion, a badminton set, using the bed as a net. We managed to kill many a rainy afternoon with this activity, as well as a few other honeymoon bedroom games that I will not go into too much detail about to save Jack's blushes. We went there in the autumn of '87; you can Wikipedia Jack's birthday and fill in the blanks.

Annoyingly, Michael had omitted to tell me that, although by all accounts he was terrible at most sports, he could play a mean game of badminton. Something that was hammered home to me on the final leg of our trip to Bird Island, where it rained even more than the other two islands we had stayed on. It was on this tiny outlier, miles from anywhere, that the torture of being repeatedly thrashed by him at badminton finally began to take its toll on my mood. I managed to just about style out these defeats with a thin veneer of good grace, but he could see that I was far from amused. My grip on pretending to be a good loser was finally lost on our last night there, when I had happened upon a Scrabble set in

the visitors' lodge, and had a thought to 'switch disciplines', as I was sick to death of the constant defeats. This was my chance to get even; it would be a battle of wits, and based on what I'd seen of Michael so far in the marriage, I felt quietly confident.

It started quite well, but as the game progressed, Michael built up an impressive lead. It was well into the game when he placed his tiles on the board and was pretty pleased with himself, as it included a triple word score, as well as a double letter score. Maybe it was all the rain, maybe it was just the long string of defeats – I don't think it was a delayed reaction to the marriage itself – but it was at this moment that I finally flipped.

'I can't believe you did that! I had a great word lined up for those squares, which meant I could have caught up with you!' I yelled at the top of my voice, over the sound of the rain beating down on the tin roof of our cabana. 'Fuck!'

'Fuck?' replied Michael drily. 'That wouldn't have fitted there.'

I could have throttled him. This was no time for joshing.

'It was my go,' he continued, clearly unaware of the magnitude of the situation. 'I'm entitled to put my tiles on any free squares. You don't own the board.'

'That's typical of you. Just doing what you please!' And with that, I slammed the board shut, threw it at his head, causing the loose tiles to fly all over the room, and stormed out into the dark, stormy night.

When I finally returned an hour or so later, drenched to the skin, I had calmed down, having had some soggy time to reflect on my being such a ridiculously bad loser. I apologised, thereby strictly adhering to my mother's pre-wedding

advice of that well-worn, oft-quoted old cliché: 'You should never let the sun go down on an argument.' Especially if you have caused it!

So, it was with a large amount of trepidation that I agreed with Michael's plan (in all honesty, that applies to most of his plans) to introduce Scrabble to our children, as a way of trying to improve their pretty ropey spelling and use of words. When it comes to education, you have to use all the tools at your disposal, even at the risk of exposing the underbelly of one of my more unseemly characteristics. Little did I know that it was actually my eldest son who would cause the bigger problem and test his father's patience to breaking point . . . I will leave him to elaborate further.

My father only decided to allow Scrabble back into our lives as he figured that it was educational (in the same way that Monopoly gives you business skills and Snakes and Ladders comes in handy if you find a cobra's nest in your attic). He figured it would help with our spelling and vocabulary. And tbf it has made my words and that well gooderer.

The problem with intergenerational Scrabble, though, is that parents, as my mother has already demonstrated, always manage to take it way too seriously. Possibly they see it as a test to find out how far they've got along the road to dementia. It's just a game! The meltdown that ensued when I once won a game by putting down the word 'waz' was absurd. What followed were hours of heated etymological debate as to whether it constituted slang or not. My father went completely AWOL, ironically another word I had already triple-word-scored with. I can see why he was annoyed with that one, especially when he asked me what

it meant and I said it was a bird that comes out at night and goes 'tu-whit tu-whoo'. It's a game whose repercussions can last for days. In the immediate aftermath, you're able to cut the tension in the villa with a knife, my father quietly seething as I try to drop 'waz' into as many conversations as I can, just to hammer home that it is a proper word. I may even have had to show my father its Wikipedia definition, just to prove its legitimacy. And for those of you thinking, 'How is "waz" classed as a word on Wikipedia?' It's because I changed it to do so. Show me someone who hasn't changed a Wikipedia entry to win an argument and I will show you a liar. Indeed, 57 per cent of people have changed an entry on Wikipedia to win an argument, according to a stat I put on Wikipedia while writing this paragraph. Anyway, he could argue till the cows came home: with my nimble Wikipedia skills, the poor sod was wazzing in the wind.

In all honesty, the games worth playing on holiday don't need boards and most certainly don't require intellect. The best games are much simpler pursuits, their main purpose whiling away the hours spent travelling in the car and possibly the added the bonus of winding everyone up around you. Here are the pound-for-pound travel game greatest hits.

Travel Games

I Spy

The OG, the GOAT, an age-old classic passed down from generation to generation. It's so old Neanderthals probably played this game on hunting trips. 'I spy with my little eye something beginning with M.' 'Mammoth – *run!*' It's the

ultimate intellectual challenge for the infant traveller. The chess of the prepubescent. Many hours have been spent the world over in planes, trains and family sedans playing this one. Staring out of windows, contemplating whether you can get away with spying 'the sky' for the tenth time that trip (always a favourite, and rightly so – requiring as it does a certain degree of lateral thinking). I Spy is glorious in its simplicity, wholesome to the core and could liven the atmosphere of even the most arduous of journeys. I bet even paramedics crack this one out every now and again to lighten the mood when they've got a particularly gory situation on the gurney and a long drive to A and E.

'I spy with my little eye something beginning with F.'

'Farm?'

'Nope.'

'Field?'

'No, come on, inside the ambulance. You really need to get this.'

'I don't know; I give up.'

'Flat-lining!'

'Oh my God, the patient's flat-lining! Why didn't you say?!'

'Your turn!'

This is why I love I Spy. It's a fun way to slip in important titbits of information about the trip, a way of playfully pointing out the odd ball your parents might have dropped.

'I spy with my little eye something beginning with C.'

'It's congestion charge, you might want to get on the phone. If only it hadn't taken you an hour to guess it; that could be an expensive brain fart.'

I guess the only word of warning is that silent letters can be a bit of a spanner in the works with this game. Twenty

minutes spent going through every word in the dictionary beginning with N before your little brother reveals the thing he's spied actually begins with a K. And where did you see a knob anyway? Oh, I'm the knob, wow. Game over.

The Alphabet Game

In the same ballpark as I Spy, this game requires a sharp mind and an eagle eye. Each of you will take turns to spot something out of the window that begins with the correct sequential letter of the alphabet, A through to Z. For example, you might start with 'A' for airport, then turn off to spot 'B' for B road, 'C' for car park, 'D' for doggers, 'E' for I think that stuff on the windscreen is eja . . . Oh no, my bad, bird poo. Shall we maybe reverse the car, Mummy? That man struggling to put his pants back on looks awfully angry.

Obviously, some letters are harder than others. You need to hope that, if you're the poor bastard that gets lumbered with X, you're driving the car at the time. That way you can take a detour via a hospital in the hope of spotting an X-ray department through the window. Either that or keep a xylophone in the glove compartment. That said, in my family I've got out of many a sticky X-situation with the help of my beloved pater and the word 'xenophobe'.

Number Plate Game

Much like poker or *Doctor Who*, there are many different incarnations of this game. Some involve using the number plate to inspire anagrams and acronyms, seeing the jumble of letters as a springboard for mind-bending linguistic

gymnastics. I think that version of the game is for the clever kids, the ones who grow up to be contestants on *Countdown*. I assume this is what life was like in the family car if your dad was Gyles Brandreth. I'm embarrassed to admit that the version of the game I used to play as a child was slightly more dumbed down. I would sit in the back of the car with a pad and pen and just write them down. No gameplay, just logging them all down like a carspotter. Essentially data entry. Pretty weird, now I look back on it. I think that's the version of the game for the kids who dream of growing up to be traffic wardens.

Rock Paper Scissors

I mean, you would have thought Rock Paper Scissors is the simplest game of them all to master but you'd be surprised. It's a game that someone who'd literally been living in a cave all their life could get to grips with pretty quickly (even if they'd probably stick to 'rock' most of the time rather than the other two new-fangled options), yet, incredibly, it manages time and again to throw up a few controversies.

'Do we draw on three or after three?' Always after!

Or the cheeky bastard who loses the game then instantly claims the international rules of Rock Paper Scissors state that it's always best of three, only to then lose again and rewrite the rule book on the spot to make it first to three instead. Utter shithousery! I even played with someone once who tried to claim that rock beat paper! It's rare that I'm rendered speechless, but this oxygen burglar announced that, in reality, a rock would be able to tear through a sheet of paper.

'Obviously,' I reasoned, 'paper has to beat rock, otherwise

the outcomes are not binary and the whole game is compromised.' That got me nowhere so I gave up without even trying to explain the scissors, an object I prayed someone with his brain capacity would never be allowed near. Actually, he gave me a Chinese burn and I went back to logging my number plates.

Not My Parents

In this hilarious game, you tell strangers that the adults dragging you through the supermarket or telling you off in an airport are not actually your mum and dad. The more intense the situation, the more points you can award yourself. For example, high scores for a border crossing or while being pulled over by a traffic cop. The only way parents can fight back is by playing the 'fake adoption revelation' card – 'look, this seems as good a time to tell you as any . . .' – in which case they score points relative to the amount of lasting psychological damage they cause. The game is best played with anyone in a uniform, although pounding on the back window of the car and mouthing to the driver next to you that you're being held against your will can bring a little levity to even the most tedious traffic jam. The ultimate winner of the game is the child that manages to get their parents put on Interpol's most wanted list.

Who Am I?

This can be a frustrating game to play, especially with elderly relatives. I mean, to be fair, if we're talking really elderly relatives 'Who am I?' can have a slightly bleaker reality, less a

parlour game and more an actual question you have to keep answering. But the standard-issue version of this game sees the group using up to twenty yes/no questions to ascertain the identity of each player. Watch out for the relatives who can't grapple with the concept of the yes/no question and get themselves disqualified immediately. Also, the dickhead who thinks they can pick multiple people. What possesses a person to select One Direction? That is not a person and therefore we have spent the last twenty minutes heading in just about every direction as this game is called 'Who Am I?' not 'Who Are We?'.

The game might also need a few ground rules set out at the start, such as clearly defining the term 'celebrity' as having to be someone that people have actually heard of. I have no doubt that Herbert Butterfield is a very respected historian, but I don't think he'd be high up on many lists drawn up by the *I'm a Celebrity Get Me Out of Here* booker. He is, therefore, a wholly inappropriate person for my father to have selected. Twenty questions? I reckon I could ask one thousand and twenty questions and I still would be no closer to working out that was who you were, Daddy!

The name game where one has to guess the identity of a person written on a Post-it note plastered to your forehead is a popular derivation of Who Am I?. In this version, names can be non-celebrities: relatives, acquaintances, work colleagues and the like. It was very popular in our household, until my father guessed that he had the name of my mother's friend Jill from her hockey team on his forehead. That would have been fine had he not guessed it by asking the question, 'Do I hate this person?'

Children: 'Yes.'

My father: 'Is it Jill?'

Deathly silence. In fairness, it wouldn't have been as bad if Jill hadn't been playing too.

The Bottle Game

Not as in 'spin the'; we're not *that* kind of family. This is a game of risk. It requires resolve, accuracy, an empty bottle, a full bladder and a steady hand on the wheel. The aim of the game is pretty self-explanatory. It demands precision and daring and possibly a trip to the car wash if you hit a speed bump or pedestrian. It's more of a solo game, as it can cause some distress among passengers . . . especially if you're travelling on public transport at the time. Big no-no! Although, to be honest, if said passengers are asleep it is possible to get away with a stealth round depending on the depth of the bottle and what kind of shallow wazzing angle you can achieve on entry. There is, of course, a fine line between the pursuit of sporting excellence and sheer exhibitionism. But if you're on a night bus, pretty much anything goes. It's worth remembering, when playing this game, that one of life's great lessons when sizing up your container is: whatever you think is big enough, add a bit more volume. Whenever you hear that statistic that 60 per cent of the body is made up of water, it always sounds a bit far-fetched, but it becomes only too real when you've thumbed yourself into an empty bottle of Lucozade on the M40 and broken the seal. Why, of all the times, has my body decided that now is the moment it wants to expel the entire 60 per cent? Why does my bladder want to wring the rest of my body out like a sponge? One other note of caution with this game: be sure to know the prior

contents of the receptacle you choose before committing. A Thermos, for example, can look appealingly capacious, but if it previously housed your mother's homemade sweet potato and chilli soup, you could be looking at a major road traffic accident and a post-mortem examination that does not paint you in the best light.

Tongue Twisters

Sally and her sea shells, Peter Piper and his pickled pepper, whatever the woodchuck guy was called (presumably Woody?): these tongue twisters are a great way to stave off boredom and improve one's elocution in the process (again, I reckon these would have been a real feature with the Brandreths). These games are also very useful if you're trying to get your parents to pull over for a pit stop. Even if they're insisting there isn't time to stop at a service station and they really must crack on, give them twenty choruses of 'Betty Botter bought a bit of butter' and those tyres will be screeching to a halt quicker than you can say, 'But a bit of better butter mixed in this batter might just make my bit of batter better.' OK, bad example. That's actually pretty hard to say.

Fantasy Dinner Party

Possibly the most middle-class game ever invented (with the exception of Spot the Avocado in the Waitrose Carrier Bag). This enjoyable conversation starter requires each family member to select the ideal guest list for their fantasy dinner party, dead or alive. Personally, I always go for guests who

are alive, as I think they give a lot more conversationally than the dead. Corpses rarely contribute. And the smell means you'll probably want to dine al fresco. Selections can be really insightful. Someone's choices say a lot about them. The respect I had for my sister went up considerably the last time we played and her first choice of guest was American abolitionist Harriet Tubman. It then instantly took a nosedive when she decided to sit Tubman next to Shane from Westlife. Don't know what they'd have to talk about – she'd probably just want to know what Louis Walsh is really like. Still, it was better than my father's line-up, which was essentially the entire front bench of Margaret Thatcher's Conservative government from 1986. Less fantasy dinner party, more fantasy Cabinet. No need to bring your own bottle, guys, the miners will throw enough at you. And my poor mother, whose guest list took a bit of a hit with Operation Yewtree. In recent games, Gary Glitter has reluctantly had to give up his seat at her fantasy dining table to Paul Hollywood. Do you wanna be in my gang, my gang, my gang? Unfortunately, not any more, Gary. So if you wouldn't mind getting your coat and maybe taking that Bay City Roller with you. Dropping like flies! For a moment, it looked like her fantasy dinner party was just going to be her and Norman Wisdom having a quiet dinner à deux, but luckily a few acquittals and the rise to fame of the nation's favourite silver-haired baker and the party can get started again.

If you want to play a real blinder, have the whole family go first, leaving them to populate their fantasy dinner parties with politicians, celebrities and disgraced pop stars. Then, when it comes to your go, take a moment to consider it before declaring that your fantasy dinner party would be

your family, you couldn't think of a group of people dead or alive you'd rather spend an evening with. Brownie points incoming (although this approach has been known to bring on abrupt bouts of travel-sickness in the siblings). OK, maybe them and Thierry Henry. And possibly Germaine Greer to stick next to Daddy – just for a laugh.

Never Have I Ever

Look, I've included it because it's a classic. But I don't know whether this is a wise game to play with the family. It's certainly a game you have to approach with a degree of caution. The Russian roulette of late-night banter. Nothing worse than one of the kids getting overexcited and trying to cheekily confuse the adults by saying, 'Never have I ever had a 69,' only to have the joke seriously backfire when Granny takes a large swig of her Bloody Mary. This is made even more disturbing when you realise Granddad's drink has remained untouched.

Literary Pursuits

The right book is, of course, important to pack in your suitcase. My father has a habit of bringing the most inappro-priate book he can to wherever we are going. Most recently we had a stand-off at Heathrow when I found a Hitler biography in his briefcase: he was about to board a flight to Munich. I honestly think I'd have been less horrified if he'd packed a bong or some Semtex. His justification that we were visiting the Eagle's Nest during our stay and therefore he wanted to brush up on a few dates and places so as not to

be 'shown up by the tour guide' held little credence with me. An impasse followed, one that culminated with me threatening to destroy the book and him telling me that's exactly the kind of thing Hitler would have done.

The point is holiday reading should be light and frothy and put you in a good mood to enable you to spend time with the family. David Jason's autobiography – fine. *Fred and Rose: The Wicked Wests of Cromwell Road* – less than ideal. My father's obsession with history books, the more morbid the better, simply doesn't put him in the right mindset for a family holiday – sitting by the pool reading a book about the Ottoman genocide, then expecting to be fun company at the dinner table.

Also, don't be the one who makes a point of how many books they've read on holiday. If you're able to read that many books, all you're doing is making it very clear just how much you hate the rest of the people you are on holiday with, and you're looking for anything to do rather than spend time with them. I'm not saying that's wrong. I'm just saying you need to be subtle about it. One book is enough, maybe two, there is always one sibling in every family, in my case my sister, who feels the need to put the slower members of the family to shame by completing an entire mobile library of books before lunch on the first day. It's not a race. She's smugly telling my mother how she's rattled through the entire *Sunday Times* Bestsellers List, while I am struggling to get out of the first chapter of *Harry Potter and the Philosopher's Stone*. I don't think she reads them properly; I've watched her and she doesn't even put her finger under the words like a normal person. She's sooo Hermione. Not that I knew that at the time, as that character doesn't appear until page 79, a

destination I never reached and something only revealed to me years later when they made the book I never managed to finish into a film. Until the age of about nineteen, I thought Harry Potter was just a story about a boy who lived in a cupboard under the stairs in the suburbs.

Medical

Your health should never be taken for granted when travelling to foreign parts, especially when you're travelling with my father. At his age, he's like a car that you are not confident will pass its MOT. You're just hoping none of the bits that are hanging off will turn out to be important. A first-aid kit should be packed containing every medicine there is on the market.

'Since my stomach surgery, I pride myself on the consistency of my bowels,' my father boasted before our trip to the Far East. Needless to say, the venue he chose for this announcement was the dinner table. Rather hard to get down Mummy's oxtail soup after that.

'I shit like clockwork.' That's a nice catchphrase, Daddy. You should put that on merch. 'And I'm always a Type Two on the Bristol Stool Chart,' he added, like this was a star sign, as I considered again whether I wanted to do this trip at all.

Then he accidentally ate tom yum soup in the first class lounge and was strapped to the lavatory for twenty-four hours, the hideous sounds emanating from his room suggesting he had definitely reached Type 7 and beyond on the Bristol Stool Chart. Incidentally, no disrespect to the people of Bristol, but I do wonder if you're putting your time to its best use. Fortunately, my mother had packed every blocker, antispasmodic, relaxer and reliever under the sun and the

crisis was averted. I took one of each with a large glass of red wine and not only could I not hear him any more, I got the best night's sleep I've ever had.

In fact, she had packed medicines for every eventuality, including bug sprays and repellents, painkillers, indigestion remedies for when I forced my father off-piste menu-wise and anti-chafing cream.

'I don't care how desperate Daddy gets, I'm not applying that!'

'It's hot over there; I don't want either of you getting scrot rot!' I should explain at this point that my mother grew up with three older brothers (and, based on the phrase 'scrot rot', apparently on a pirate ship), so she is no stranger to the male vernacular or, it seemed, to male medical requirements in hot countries.

I was well stocked with my mother's favourite go-to cure-all Sudocrem, which she slaps on anything and everything like a medical version of WD-40, and, most bizarrely of all, condoms, which was extremely unnerving bearing in mind we were going away on a father-and-son trip to Thailand. What did she think we were going to be getting up to? The most positive interpretation I can come up with is she thought we might want to smuggle some drugs back.

It's not just far-flung territories that one has to be medically prepared for; even a hop across the Channel can be fraught with danger. My father's stomach kicking off in the Côte d'Azur was no laughing matter. What fun it was to watch a French doctor attempt to explain to him in broken English what suppository medication entailed. A clumsy analogy about the Channel Tunnel may have been the moment he was tipped over the edge.

'The pervert wanted me to put it up my derrière! Typical of the French!'

He then spent the rest of the trip pondering out loud why the French were so obsessed with putting medicine up their bottoms rather than swallowing it, concluding that it was probably to keep their mouths free for smoking.

What you don't pack is nearly as important as what you do. I travel light, as they say, which I don't think is anything to be ashamed of. In the era of budget airlines – which, according to Daddy, is any that offers New World wines in first class – overpacking is a cardinal and costly sin. No one wants to be the family member that has gone over their allotted baggage allowance. Especially if the head of your party has packed an eight-hundred-page hardback biography of Hitler and still sailed on through.

Standing in the Ryanair queue, you go through your suitcase to see which items can be skimmed, crushed into your sibling's bag or worn, as a final solution (probably shouldn't say that quite so close to a reference to Hitler). We've all at some point suffered the ignominy of having to board a plane late, clothed in every jacket we own, waddling down the aisle looking like the Michelin Man and trying to avoid every judgemental eye contact cast our way from beneath the peaks of three baseball caps.

One has to admire the resilience on display, and the lengths British people in particular will go to to avoid paying £10 per kilo for additional luggage. I've seen people nearly pass out from exhaustion, attempting to cram their wheelie bag into that little cage that determines whether it's small enough to be deigned hand luggage or not. Men stopping

just short of bringing out welding apparatus to bend the metallic ribs of the frame to their will. It's the second big ritual of the British holiday experience, and people might be even better at it were it not for the first big ritual – hammering the Stellas in the airport Spoons.

But we are determined. 'I'm not giving Ryanair any more of my fucking money,' we grunt, while attempting a manoeuvre as futile as trying to push a turkey through a letter box. Give my mother a bag of any size, the impetus of saving money and a tub of her trusty Sudocrem and she's like the masked figure that demonstrates the games on *The Cube*: that bag's in that cage before they've done the first call.

It's long been my opinion that when the CEO of Ryanair, Michael O'Leary, dies, it would be a little bit of poetic justice if they put him in a coffin and then dug a plot for his grave that was just too small for the coffin to fit into. I'd like his departing moments to be spent with one of his employees desperately trying to cram his coffin into the ground – maybe opening it up to see if there are any bits that his relatives can carry away with them – all so that the O'Leary estate doesn't have to pay an additional burial charge.

What Not to Pack

You mustn't take stupid items. You're going to stay in a hotel; they will have towels. Every hotel has towels. Even Crazy Jack's Roadside Hooker & Homicide Motel will have something for the drifters to dry their hands on after they've shanked you. Most hotels don't just have towels, they are museums to the art of towelling. In fact, the hotel bathroom will be made almost entirely of towels; there's practically

one for each limb, you could mummify yourself with the amount of towels they provide. There will be different shapes of towel, and sizes that you will never see at any other time in your life; the one that's somewhere between a foot towel and a flannel is only ever found in hotel bathrooms. What it's used for is one of life's great mysteries, like the reason they built Stonehenge or what Canada is actually for. We've all tried to wrap it around our waist only for it to not quite reach round and flutter open at the back like a hospital gown, exposing your soaking arse crack to a nice cold draught.

You will not be able to move for towels, so don't feel the need to pack your own. Turning up to a hotel with your own towel is like bringing your own knife and fork to a restaurant: it's off-the-spectrum levels of weird. Needless to say, at some point I fully expect my parents to start packing their own towels. And now I come to think of it, on several occasions in the Far East, my father took his own knife and fork to restaurants.

This brings me neatly to my next piece of advice when packing: make sure you leave plenty of room for stolen hotel items. While arriving with a towel is not OK, leaving with one most certainly is. It adds an air of devil-may-care highway robbery to even the most humdrum night in an Ibis. Make sure you have reserved space, maybe even an entire spare suitcase, to clear out every item you can from that hotel room. There is no shame in paying excess baggage to cover the cost of smuggling home a stolen bath mat or a couple of pillows. More on this later.

It's not just towels that I put on the packing black list; there are other items that should be cast from your parents

suitcases, like suits. The whole point of going away on a holiday is that you don't have to wear a suit. Especially children. I don't care if it's a nice restaurant, we are not going out dressed like we're at a royal wedding. We're in the Mediterranean. Anyone wearing a suit is probably a member of a crime syndicate. We do not want to end the evening being invited to kiss the ring of the Godfather.

My father will wear a suit in any temperature, no matter where in the world we are.

'Good God, I'm sweating like a nun in a field of cucumbers.'

'Yes, Daddy – setting that analogy aside – that's because we're in Bangkok and you're wearing a suit.'

'It's linen, Jack.'

I think old men think linen is some magical fabric that is impenetrable to the sun. I assume they watch Premiership footballers wearing breathable clothing specially designed to keep them as cool and sweat free as possible in the heat of the action, and think, 'Well, they'd be a lot better off if those football shirts were made of linen.' Linen is not magical; you're still wearing a suit and you will pass out from heatstroke unless you take off your jacket!

'What? And let the locals see me with sweat patches? I'm an Englishman, Jack, not a beast!'

While I think it's ridiculous for a dad to wear a suit on holiday, under no circumstances whatsoever do I want him to suddenly start dressing like he's a teenager. A T-shirt is just about acceptable, but just as every father has to have that tricky conversation with his son about the birds and the bees (which in my case was an excruciating reworking of the classic that involved extra details about an older bee that had bagged itself a much younger bird by showing it

a lot of honey), there comes a time in every son's life when he has to call his father into a room and have the awkward 'shorts conversation'. Namely, that he should never wear them again, especially the skimpy turquoise abomination to which my father has already confessed to degrading his sartorial reputation with. The time in your life when experimentation like that was acceptable has passed. You may think the locals don't want to see you in shirtsleeves, but I assure you it's preferable to them seeing you walk down the beach in shorts, thereby exposing them to legs that look like a plate of condemned veal, criss-crossed with varicose veins that, at a glance, make them look like a map of the London Underground, albeit a map with a blue line that heads north and terminates at somewhere that sounds even less appealing than Cockfosters.

Other parental items that should be put into the metaphorical wheelie bag 101 are, in no particular order: those French Legionnaires caps with the weird flap at the back to protect your neck from the sun but actually make you look like a Basset Hound. You're not in the army, and if you are over the age of five, you will look ridiculous. Any kind of sunglasses that clip on to a pair of spectacles; any convenience this may offer is massively outweighed by how much of a tit you look. Crocs, enough said. Any glasses or sunglasses that are on a chain or string. Any kind of slogan or comical non-age-appropriate T-shirt or hoodie. Phone holsters that attach to your belt. Crocs again, just to be absolutely clear. Hawaiian shirts. Finally – and this shouldn't really need saying, but I shall say it nonetheless – budgie smugglers. The only people who are allowed to wear budgie smugglers are Frenchmen and elite athletes ... and maybe wrestlers. If you do not fall

into one of these categories, you are categorically prohibited from wearing them. Especially if you have one of those dad bods with a paunch that sits over and obscures large swathes of the bathing costume, so that to the casual observer you appear to be striding down a heavily populated beach naked.

However, above all else, when it comes to holidaying with your parents, there is one item that must be addressed. An item so offensive if found in your parents' possession, you are well within your rights to take it, burn it, have the ashes compacted into a diamond, attach the diamond to a rocket and then fire it into space. Even then, I'd think you were possibly underreacting.

That item is the abominable fanny pack, an accessory that was designed in a factory somewhere, probably Germany (I don't want to sound too much like Michael Whitehall, but it has all the hallmarks of their diabolical cunning), with the sole purpose of being deployed by parents to embarrass their children as much as is humanly possible.

Let me say right now, for the record, there is absolutely no – and I repeat *no* – practical reason to wear a fanny pack. Trousers have pockets, and when they are found wanting, the backpack has stepped up to the plate. Why now, while abroad, are we suddenly desperate to put our valuables in a garish, zip-up pouch and have them dangle from our midriff, like a nylon udder? It makes you immediately identifiable as a tourist. All the locals know how to spot the holidaymakers: they're the ones who look as though their valuables have prolapsed out of them.

There is some flimsy argument doing the rounds that the fanny pack has some kind of safety function: having your valuables hovering above your crotch is a more thief-proof

option, as no mugger would want to go through the social awkwardness of having to rip it off your nether regions. Firstly, one thing I have always observed about muggers is that they're not generally constrained by notions of social awkwardness. They are not the sort of people who would consider committing theft, but then decide against it on the basis that it might involve a faux pas. Secondly, to the people who champion this argument, I would posit this, a question which it should take you nanoseconds to answer: would you rather a) have all your valuables stolen? Or b) be seen in public with a fanny pack? If you answer b, not only should you not go on holiday, but the people responsible for your care should not really be letting you leave the house.

The only thing worse than the item itself is, of course, its name. It's like it's been designed specifically to deliver the maximum amount of embarrassment possible to the child of the parent wearing it; double-barrelled shame. Given my father's love of innuendo coupled with my mother's fondness for vaginal banter, the fanny pack is like a red rag to a pair of old perverts.

So not only is it visually offensive, it is also an excuse for parents to say the word 'fanny' in front of their children with a wanton disregard for how traumatising that might be. More than a wanton disregard – I'd go so far as to call it a cavalier delight. It's like when a father sees 'faggots' on the menu and uses it as a pass to say the word as many times as possible and make his snowflake children feel uncomfortable. And when I say 'a father', you of course realise I mean 'my father'.

No boy should ever have to hear his own father utter the sentence, 'I'm just going to have a rootle in Mummy's fanny pack.'

In the interest of balance and so that we don't get too many complaints from the International Society of Fanny Packers, my mother wanted to add this. It is a strange hill she has chosen to die on. . .

Hilary: IN DEFENCE OF THE FANNY PACK

I feel it's incumbent upon me, as a result of Jack's vociferous trashing of the fanny pack, to mount a robust defence of not just one of my holiday essentials but to my mind one of the world's most valuable inventions. Long, long before Tim Berners-Lee invented the World Wide Web, Fleming discovered penicillin and even earlier than when Galileo first saw the craters and mountains on the moon, I feel sure that our forebears would have fashioned animal skins into a pouch worn around their midriff in order to carry their tools while they hunter-gathered and to protect them from a Stone Age mugging or unexpected mammoth attack. And lo, the fanny pack was born.

I think that Jack's protestations are a bit disingenuous, as I reckon secretly he wishes he had the confidence and panache, not to say the hips, to carry one off. Many's the time he has been saved by an essential emergency item from the cavernous nether regions of my fanny pack (I can imagine him squirming as he reads those words, because he knows it's true!).

I have been known on occasions to wear more than one at a time – double bagging, as it were – so as to get more fanny for my buck, creating what I think of as a very fetching

double-decker or mezzanine effect. I also have to factor in that Michael is likely to say to me once we are far from home that he 'doesn't want to ruin the line of his jacket by carrying his stuff in his pockets' and could he slip something of his into my 'fanny'. Does it have enough room for his valuables? Well, Michael Whitehall packs quite a lot in the valuables department I can tell you; we are talking glasses, fountain pens, leather diaries, on dressier occasions even his Prince Albert, a fob watch he inherited from his father, an item Jack for some reason finds even more disturbing than my fanny pack. Suffice to say, Michael's odds and sods would fill a whole fanny pack with ease, hence my requirement to carry more than one.

Their fundamental role is the same, namely to ensure that I am never separated from any of my arsenal of crucial holiday items, for when travelling I am like a human Swiss Army Knife. My lieutenant in chief, the humble wet wipe, guaranteed to get any hard-pressed mother out of all sorts of scrapes; the trusty tissue; my old friend Miss Lip Salve; a back-up credit card; a dog poo bag (even if we are travelling without a dog – you never know); the five-pound note (Michael says you never know when the Euro will flat-line, so we should always carry some currency that's actually built to last); a biro; the mini torch (in an ideal world these two items are combined into one mighty multi-tool) two paracetamols; four Rennies; a pair of spare contact lenses for Jack (he is as blind as a bat without them, but he won't invest in some sensible glasses-attached-to-a-string); blister plasters; a hair tie; sunglasses; and of course our modern-day hand-held computer (and camera), the mobile phone. In the old days, that selection of items would have required a large

backpack, with its attendant crumpled beneath its weight. I would therefore argue that the humble fanny pack is in fact good for our health and has probably saved our hard-pressed and overworked NHS millions, not to mention preventing 'lost work days'. When first patented, it must have been the Pfizer vaccine of its day. So, unless Jack has a better solution for the conveyance of these vital items, I suggest he buttons it when it comes to his opinions on the fanny pack and just admits that my fanny is actually a thing of beauty, a bearer, protector and giver of life.

I'm literally speechless. To be honest, I couldn't make it to the end of that bit. Let's just pretend that never happened.

Planes, Trains and Horse-Drawn Carts

Aeroplanes

'THEY WON'T LEAVE without us,' has always been my philosophy when it comes to air travel. One that always stood me in good stead. Until they did.

Most travel days start with the mad dash to the airport. Parents like to leave an unfeasibly long amount of time to arrive for a flight, shaking you violently from your sleep at 4 a.m.

'Chop, chop. We should have left ten minutes ago; we're really cutting it fine.'

'But our flight's not till seven o'clock tonight.'

'Yes, but we need to be there in good time.'

'How are we getting to the airport? On foot? Sedan chair? We could ride sloths there, Mummy, and still be in enough time to enjoy a comprehensive security pat-down and browse.'

The taxi journey to the airport invariably descends into a scene that's a cross between *The Fast and the Furious* and *Driving Miss Daisy*, the driver veering across the road, speedily weaving his way through the traffic, as your mother grunts thinly veiled threats into his ear, urging him to bypass the traffic by mounting the kerb – a few pedestrians mowed down happily chalked up as collateral damage. The number of holidays we've been on, it's amazing there's anyone left alive in Hounslow.

In the good old days of the pre-ordered taxi – or, in my parents' case, the cheaper alternative of the pre-ordered local minicab (the adverts are right – it literally was just a stranger's car) – this journey was a mild irritation, but with the relatively recent introduction of Uber, it's an ordeal with much more far-reaching consequences. As most parents don't have Uber accounts (you might as well ask them how often they use Grindr), it's normally left to an offspring to book the car to the airport on *their* account. As users of the service will know, Uber works on a rating system where both the driver and the passenger are rated by each other. A high passenger rating ensures a speedy pick-up in the future. Therefore, cultivating and maintaining a high rating is very important. I'm proud to say I rock 4.9 stars, a rating I have cultivated through hard work, a degree of charm and sucking up to every driver whose car I enter. I like to think that when I leave the vehicle, the driver sighs gently to themselves and says, 'What a delightful ride. Just the pleasure of that young man's company has made my whole day – indeed, the whole of my chosen career – worthwhile. Five stars for him.' All this good work goes out of the window when you have to incorporate the serious reputational liability of my

father's personality, a man troubled by neither self-doubt nor self-awareness. I remember one occasion, when we were very late for a flight and racing to the airport in an Uber booked on my account, the driver started driving down a cul-de-sac. My father snapped, 'First time in a car, is it?'

To everyone's surprise, the driver snapped back and started having a pop at my father – asked him what his problem was, right in front of me. A full-blown argument broke out in the car. I'm afraid I had no choice but to stand up for the person I cared most about.

'How dare you speak to him like that? Michael, apologise to Rafik immediately.'

Yes, I'm not ashamed to admit it: I stood up for the driver over my own father, as I cared more about my Uber rating than my father's honour.

So, in my humble opinion, it's probably better to opt for public transport over an Uber if you want to minimise stress and keep your Uber rating intact when getting to the airport. Even if you will have to put up with Michael Whitehall repeatedly asking why the Piccadilly line doesn't have a first-class dining carriage.

Security

Another element of any airport departure that, if you will excuse the unfortunate choice of word, is guaranteed to hijack you timewise is the dreaded airport security. Actual Jihadis probably feel less nervous in the queue for the X-ray machine than someone travelling with Michael Whitehall. Always try to give older relatives a little refresher on the protocols before you arrive at the airport. It baffles me that

no matter how many times they go through security, they behave like it's alien to them. It's pretty much the same experience at the supermarket with a self-service checkout. On a point of principle, they will feel the need to act like they've just been roused from a twenty-year coma.

'Didn't have to go through all this nonsense when I was your age,' says my father every time we go through the exact same procedures he has now been doing for over two decades.

'Yes, but that was before terrorism existed, Daddy. The most likely thing to bring down a plane when you were my age was a Messerschmitt.'

'You know whose fault this is? That bloody shoe bomber!' my father will bellow at the top of his voice, as he struggles to take off a tightly laced Church's brogue, still adamant the slip-on was not a better choice that morning.

'Don't say shoe bomber in an airport, please,' I hiss, as a security man eyes my father's gouty toe as though it's a suspect package.

'If it hadn't been for that bloody shoe bomber, we could keep our shoes on; but no, thanks to Richard Reid, we now have to go through this farce every time we fly to make sure we're not shoe bombers.'

'Stop saying shoe bomber, for God's sake!' By this point everyone else in the queue is staring at us. Some of them are taking photographs.

'So now my freedom of speech is being taken away, along with my brogues—'

'The only thing being taken away will be anything they find after a full body-cavity search if you keep saying "shoe bomber" in an airport.'

'DO I LOOK LIKE A TERRORIST?'

Another thing never to say in an airport.

Also, given that he can't remember his own postcode, how the hell does he remember the name of the shoe bomber?

If you can make it through security without your father getting you all put on a no-fly list, you've then got to deal with the flight itself.

Boarding

The amazing thing is that no matter how much time you do leave, it seems there is no way to avoid the mad rom-com-style dash to actually get on the plane. Someone will have lost their boarding pass (or passport, in my case) or not heard the flight being called or spent too long in Dixons Travel bingeing on continental adaptors. Or, and this is a favourite of my father's, never a man to be 'hurried along', even for a departing plane, forgotten that the gate is deceptively far away. 'Departing from Gate 7' sounds close enough. Nope, of course it's not. It turns out Gate 7 is a short walk, then an escalator, then a shuttle, then a longer walk, then a series of travellators, through a secret passage you access by pulling a book out of a shelf, a short camel trek across the runway, down some stairs, up a waterfall and you're there. I've seen people at Gate 7 sending postcards back to passengers in the main terminal.

And of course with every step, my father cheers the journey along with comments like, 'We're halfway there! Maybe we can ask the airline for some of our money back, seeing as we've walked most of the fucking way to France already!'

As if to neg you as well along the way, there are always

electronic boards displaying '20-minute walk to Gate 7'. What would be more helpful for my family is if they could extend the message on the boards.

'20-minute walk to Gate 7. 40 minutes if you're lumbered with a 70-year-old wearing a pair of Church's brogues with a slightly gouty foot stuffed into them and a mother struggling under the weight of six fanny packs strapped in various places around her body like the buckaroo horse.'

It's on this slow walk of shame that my mother always helpfully says, 'I told you to wear your slip-ons, Michael.'

'Slip-on shoes? Don't be ridiculous, Hilary. I only ever wear proper shoes when I am out in public.'

'Out in public? We're going on holiday, Michael, not having dinner at the Garrick Club,' she replies, as she strides off purposefully towards the gate, knowing she needs the head start to begin the time-consuming process of working out which fanny pack she put the boarding passes in.

'Don't worry, Daddy, when we get to the airport in Nice the gate is really close to the exit.' And it's true the gate is right next to the exit of the airport; the only problem is we've flown with a budget airline and their version of 'Nice' is technically in Italy.

Seating

The more frugal parent will get around the problem of unreserved seating by purchasing a single speedy boarding pass, then nominating one family member to get on to the plane before everyone else and reserve four seats for the rest of the family – greedy boarding, I like to call it. It's a bit like being a canary in a coalmine, except where everyone else

in the coalmine hates the canary and thinks the canary and their whole canary family are a load of selfish bastards. I've been nominated for this task many times, in my capacity as eldest son and being generally seen by Daddy as the most dispensable member of the family, unless, at some point in the future, he needs an organ donated. It's horrendous having to sprawl across a row of seats like you're a member of Extinction Rebellion glued to the Shell head office. Lying there in shame as the rest of the passengers try to dislodge you with tuts.

'I'm so sorry these seats are taken,' you say sheepishly, as the entire plane fills up, your family always managing to be the last people to board, just to ensure that every single person on the plane despises you. I honestly think we'd get a better reception if we were actual hijackers. The next two hours of the flight are then spent constantly bickering among ourselves, as the rest of the passengers look on and wonder why on earth we were so desperate to sit together in the first place.

So, my advice is not to bother. I think the unreserved seating rule should be seen as a blessing, a convenient and diplomatic way around not having to sit together. We've got a whole fortnight ahead of us to poison each other with our personalities; let's keep some of that powder dry. Let's face it, being crammed next to anyone in an uncomfortable seat in a metal sky cage is always going to be a feat of patience. You start to get annoyed by the tiniest of things. Even your brother's breathing pattern can start to feel like nails on a chalkboard. And three hours sandwiched between my parents orating a live audio of a duty free magazine they have no intention of actually buying anything

from, I think even Buddha would find himself gritting his teeth and eyeing up the drinks trolley or that red handle on the emergency exit.

Entertainment

Movies are a useful way of passing the time on a plane and can really reduce the risks posed by prolonged interaction with your travel companions. Though selection is key. I once tucked into *Toy Story 3*, a nice easy-going kids' film, I thought, no sweat at all. Two hours and one existential crisis later: cut to me bawling my eyes out and having to pretend to the air hostess who was asking me if I was OK that I had a fear of flying and her asking the person next to me if he minded holding my hand for landing. As it was my father, he refused, saying he'd avoided being a touchy-feely parent for three decades and wasn't going to start now. Looking back on it, I'm slightly embarrassed about my behaviour. Andy had to grow up and go to college, after all, and . . . I'm sorry, I'm going again.

The other time I've been embarrassed by the in-flight entertainment was the time I saw someone in front of me watching my stand-up special. I literally caught sight of myself on his screen out of the corner of my eye. I bashfully shifted in my seat. This was a pretty cool moment; you know you've truly made it when someone is watching your jokes at 30,000 feet. I don't know if my jokes are funnier at high altitude, the way booze gets you drunk faster? Maybe, I mused, I'll go over and say hello to my superfan and make his day. I then watched him calmly lift his finger to the screen, switch me off and put on the inflight map. How bad a review is that? He deemed my stand-up so boring, he would

rather watch an animation of a little plane travelling over a map for five hours.

Some people choose to forgo the entertainment altogether and instead opt for drugs to help them get through the flight. Smoking a little joint before take-off can really help it breeze by, though make sure you choose the right place to light up – it can make the security queue even more of a hassle. I was also once advised by a mate to take Valium. I think she meant for the flight, but it might just have been for dealing with my parents in general. Still, I thought it was worth a shot to see what all the fuss was about. It didn't end well: it definitely sent me off to sleep but its strength – and possibly the Bloody Mary I washed it down with – put me into such a deep slumber that I woke up drooling and full on spooning the man next to me, gently purring into his ear. The man was furious, shouting for the air marshal and using all manner of curse words.

Not language befitting a pilot.

Hilary: DON'T DO DRUGS, KIDS

I once got some pharmaceutical advice from an antenatal-group pal. We were taking one of our first holidays having launched into parenthood. Jack was three, Molly was nearly two and I was pregnant with Barnaby, and for some inexplicable reason, we had decided to take a New Year break to Barbados. Though knowing Michael, it was probably because he'd got wind that the controller of ITV was staying there and had some availability on fully furnished villas up his backside.

Anyway, my antenatal-group friend was from America, a nation that tends to have a pill for every occasion, and she said that she had taken many transatlantic flights with her little ones and had got the whole thing down pat. Drugs were the only answer, she had confidently told me. This seemed obvious – what surprised me was that she meant for the children rather than for me.

'A teaspoon of Phenergan, which is only a mild antihistamine, given to them as you take off and they will sleep for most of the flight. Easy. Job done.'

My need to do due diligence wasn't as honed as it is now, but I did the best research I could – in a pre-internet world, I took a straw poll of my friends, asked various members of our extended family, many of whom were in the medical profession, and came down on the side of yes, it probably wouldn't do any harm.

My recollection is that no one suggested that we should try it out on a night before the flight to see whether it was suitable for our toddlers, rather than jumping straight in at the deep end of amateur pharmacology. I didn't realise that for a very tiny percentile of people who take the drug, its effects could be the total opposite of what you are hoping to achieve. Predictably for us, there was obviously a common denominator in our children's genetic make-up, which put both Jack and Molly on the 'hyped-up' end of the spectrum. We didn't have the term 'air rage' back then, so had to settle for Michael's (repeatedly barked) phrase of 'annoying little bastards'. Because for the entire journey, we were run ragged, both of us with our hands full, and in my case a belly full, literally, running up and down the aisles of the plane chasing after the two of them, at one point practically prising

their hands off some cockpit controls and trying to keep the decibels down as they merrily sang their way repeatedly through endless verses of 'The Wheels on the Bus' for the entire flight. Thank goodness the milk they give you for your coffee is UHT or those looks would definitely have curdled it. At one point, the man in front of the children lost it and could be overheard muttering, 'We're not even on a fucking bus!' Jack's hasty pivot to a remix of 'The Wings on the Plane' did very little to appease him.

Unfortunately, there was no way in these circumstances that we could have adopted our subsequent 'hit and run' policy when they were teenagers and had perpetrated some hideous misdemeanour where we would simply say, 'I'm sorry but these aren't our children,' while walking off in the opposite direction. That certainly got us out of a few scrapes in customs.

Twenty-nine years later, Michael and I were returning from an interesting trip on the *Minerva*, a cruise ship that specialised in educational, adult-only cruises (not that kind of adult-only!). They had asked Michael to do some after-dinner speaking to the passengers, as entertainment rather than for academic or instructive purposes, although I would have thought it was always educational for others to experience Michael – it's certainly taught me a thing or two. In return for this we would get a free trip. I had managed to engineer us on to the Cuba to Bermuda via the Turks and Caicos Islands leg of their meander around the world, as I had always wanted to go to Cuba. Quite an achievement, given that Michael thinks a trip to Salcombe is bordering on being too far and Jack hadn't licked him into shape on the travel front by then. He also had rather a lot of objections

to the privations of life under Cuba's communist regime, describing it on more than one occasion as, 'Liverpool but with cigars'.

The most eventful part of the trip was on the flight home from Bermuda. After a two-week cruise and four delightful nights on the island, we were definitely ready to head home, and I was ready never to hear another joke from Michael referring to my bikini bottoms as 'The Bermuda Triangle, where sailors come to die'. We boarded the plane and took our seats – booked with extra legroom right by the galley, with the steward sitting opposite and facing us. Our plan was drinks, dinner, sleep. Post take-off the dinner service duly began. We were quickly off-piste as we sank not our usual one but two large G and Ts, and it was at this point that we unfortunately hit a very 'aggressive' pocket of turbulence, resulting in the captain coming on to the PA system and telling the stewards to suspend the dinner service and return to their seats until further notice. This turned out to be the last time we heard from him, as the turbulence persisted. I assume he was wrestling with it, but he may just have bailed out and left the rest of us to our chances. After fifteen minutes, Michael turned to me and said, 'I'm going to forget about dinner and just go to sleep,' as he popped a sleeping pill into his mouth.

'Think I'm going to hang on a bit longer; you really shouldn't take them on an empty stomach,' I replied hopefully.

Half an hour later we were still being bounced around in the sky when our steward, who was still strapped in his seat facing us, caught my eye. He looked calm, which reassured

me. The last thing you want to see is the air crew panicking or, even worse, praying.

'Is this normal?' I asked him.

'Sadly yes at this time of year,' he replied. 'I don't think we'll be getting dinner out this evening,' he added.

'I might as well take my sleeping pill then,' I said, taking out the pill box. It was at this point that Michael interjected.

'This is a nightmare and that bloody pill hasn't done the job,' he said, as he leant over, picked up my pill and popped it into his mouth.

'You don't mind, do you? You operate so much better on no sleep than I do.' It seemed futile to disagree, as he had already swallowed the pill. I did wonder about the wisdom of popping two sleepers on a stomach lined only with gin, but I figured he'd be OK.

It was only twenty minutes later, when he started shivering and moaning that he was 'cold, so cold', that I began to get worried. This was the beginning of a lengthy period of strange behaviour from Michael, somewhat reminiscent of Ewan McGregor's performance in that film *Trainspotting*. I wrestled a blanket around him, in an attempt to swaddle him into inactivity. It gave him the appearance of a monk, though one not exhibiting much peace or serenity whatsoever. Then he entered a more performative stage of his psychosis.

He suddenly jolted forward and shouted at the top of his voice, 'The arms are trying to get me. Get the arms off me!' while flailing around at some imaginary assailant that he thought was sitting behind him. I dread to think what the passenger who was actually sitting behind him must have made of it, but I wasn't about to include him in this unfolding

medication-induced horror story. I've always followed the golden rule that a problem shared is a problem made much worse. The steward looked most concerned by Michael's performance, given that he was literally strapped into a front row seat. He leant forward to politely enquire, 'Does he need any help?'

'He's taken two sleeping pills and is obviously having a bad reaction. But I'm sure he'll be fine,' I replied, in that wonderful way that we Brits have of understating things and trying to appear relaxed and totally in control when we find ourselves in the middle of a shit-show. I think in reality I was trying to reassure myself as much as the steward.

'Well, keep a close eye on him and let me know if you want any help.' Hard not to keep an eye on Michael – everyone in the cabin was staring at him.

Michael's hallucinatory shenanigans lasted pretty much the entire six-hour flight and I spent a lot of time trying to shroud him from view with a blanket, as he croaked about going home in a scene straight out of *ET*. At various points, I even had to physically restrain him in his seat, when the imaginary assailants that were trying to molest him started getting the upper hand. I finally managed to cajole him sufficiently awake to have some tea and toast (the turbulence having finally subsided) while he whispered to me about how he had had a terrible night, having been constantly 'attacked by demons'. In all honesty, this was not the first time Michael has reminded me of Richard III.

When we landed in London, he was still very disorientated and didn't quite know where we were as I led him, zombie-like, through the airport. I have to say, I was both concerned

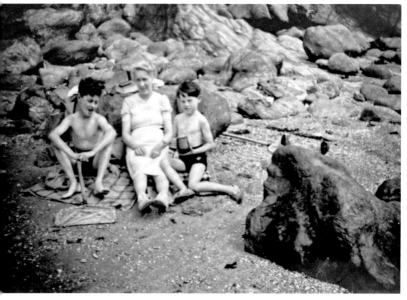

Glad Nora got us down to the beach bright and early to secure this spot.

Michael in 1958 'cracking onto a few birds' on holiday

Lord Fellowes and Michael with a Greek fisherman: the binoculars were
to keep an eye out for the fashion police.

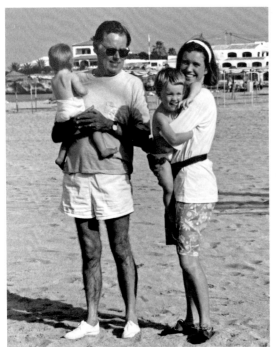

Apparently this attire was
acceptable in the '80s.

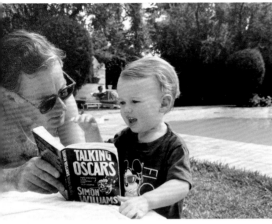

Michael's attempts to subtly influence my career path started at a very early age.

Before Instagram and Snapchat, you had to make your own filters.

'Hello, sailor!'

Contemplating the fun I could have with an ice-cold glass of water

You can't escape your genes . . .

. . . or your big brother on holiday!

Guess which one of us had the short attention span?

The beach bod went rapidly downhill from here.

Show business never sleeps but can be deployed to avoid boring
family lunches and outings to the beach.

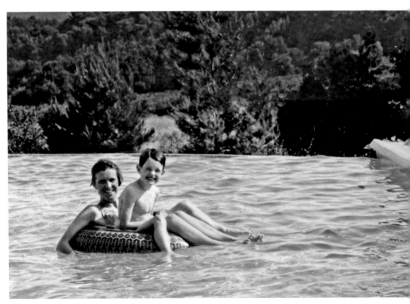

Goading Michael from the deep end

Relaxed research for holiday homework

Needed more length: both my shot and those blue monstrosities Daddy was wearing.

An early big tick off the bucket list

Binge Britain

and enjoying the uncharacteristic peace and quiet, and it also meant I was able to get on to public transport without him kicking up a fuss, the only upside of this debacle.

Note to self: This is why you should never hide ecstasy tablets in your mother's washbag.

Trains

Trains can be just as stressful as air travel. A journey home from the Edinburgh Fringe Festival with my mum and dad will live long in the memory to illustrate this. We thought we'd secured a table for the three of us, but just as the train crept out of Waverley Station a stranger wedged himself into the window seat next to my father. My mum, as usual, didn't want to make the stranger feel left out, so she made the fatal error of asking him if he'd 'had a good festival'. Six hours later, as we pulled into King's Cross, it honestly felt like we'd seen every show at the Fringe. This random crasher also went big on the snacks; I think it was the moment he split open a grab bag of Quavers and told Daddy to 'tuck in' that I realised we might never travel by train as a family again.

The sleeper train, in particular, is one that I have discovered to be a fool's paradise. The Eastern & Orient Express looks classy in the brochure, a luxury hotel on wheels. In actual fact, it is more like a padded cell on a tumble dryer. No amount of fine furnishing can make up for the fact that you are sleeping close enough to feel the occupant of the adjacent couchette (which I believe is French for 'prison bunk') breath on your eyeballs. Or any other exhalations that may occur during the night. The prospect of being in such close

proximity to any family member in this kind of situation is just too intense. I love my father, but not enough to be sealed with him in the equivalent of a Tupperware container filled with each other's BO. The thought of going to the toilet in the middle of the night is not a comforting one. It was just such a moment in Thailand, as our train gently trundled on to the bridge over the River Kwai (wonderful engineering, evidence of what us Brits can do when we actually set our minds to it, except when it comes to Hammersmith Bridge) that I let out a fart I thought I could trust. It was followed by an ominous rumble that was either my father waking from his sleep or the bridge collapsing for a second time in its short but turbulent history. I think, knowing what I know now, the destruction of the bridge may have made for a less trying night.

Horse-Drawn Carts

Indigenous transportation can be a mixed bag. A horse-drawn cart in Romania seemed like a novel way to enter into the rusticity of our surroundings; it proved to be a rather traumatic experience. I will allow Michael to explain. Any fans of animal rights or Romanian readers that haven't already been lost, you might want to skip to the next section . . .

Michael: ROMANIA

An extremity of mine that took a bashing when I was filming *Travels with My Father* with Jack in northern Romania was my wrist.

We had travelled for hours and had had quite an emotional day filming in a location with the unlikely name of The Merry Cemetery, an oxymoron if ever I heard one. Unless you've been obliged to attend a funeral for someone you don't like – a client that's fired you, perhaps, or one of your wife's friends, maybe. What had started as a larky trawl through the brightly coloured, painted tombstones depicting the often comical lives of the citizens buried there had taken a more serious turn, when we found ourselves talking about death and the meaning of life: hardly comedy gold for a light-hearted travelogue (although, given Jack was involved, the chances of comedy gold were always something of a 'hit and hope' operation). So, the director had decided to lighten things up a bit at the end of the day and thought it would be fun for Jack and me to ride off into the sunset on a horse and cart driven by a character in traditional dress.

Half an hour or so later, up turned our transport of delight, and we were loaded aboard for our final sequence of the day, before the long drive back to our hotel and our anticipated dinner. I always find talking about death really helps me work up an appetite, the way some people, I believe, find with swimming. To say that the cart wasn't in its first flush of youth was an understatement; neither was the driver, who looked like he'd just been dug up from the cemetery, and not necessarily the Merry one.

We had also, by now, picked up the local shouter. These people are a common occurrence when filming: individuals desperately trying to get themselves into any shot and hopefully into conversation with us, so as to notch up an appearance on television. Given that we already have one loudmouth whose interjections add nothing to proceedings

in the shape of my co-host, they are always surplus to requirements. Often they just want some money to go away; if only the same could be said of Jack. They always require the attentions and people-management skills of several crew members, who attempt to distract them (I've suggested the use of a cattle prod, but apparently this isn't 'woke'), while the rest of us attempt to get the scene done without their participation. So, with the shouter otherwise engaged, we headed towards the distant mountains, as the sun started to set on the horizon. Beautiful. Our director was smelling a BAFTA. I was smelling manure, but this was largely unavoidable given that we were, as I've mentioned, in Romania.

We turned a corner, thereby taking us out of shot, so Jack tapped the driver on the shoulder and attempted to signal for him to turn around, not easy given that the driver spoke no English and Jack and I spoke no Romanian. After a minute of some pretty wild gesticulating, the driver got the hang of the request. He pulled sharply on the reins and the horse suddenly found a fresh burst of energy. It swung round with such force and speed that it caused the cart to collapse into two, hurling Jack and me up into the air and on to the road (I can't imagine this had been deliberate, though I had been talking for some time about Romanian migration to the UK, and Jack claims I mentioned accordions). I had put my hand out to break my fall and felt a stabbing pain as it made contact with the road. Jack was convinced I had been killed and was mightily relieved when he heard a string of swear words. We were out of sight and earshot of the crew, so were unable to call for help. It was up to Jack and the driver to haul the cart into some sort of workable order, while I sat on the

verge nursing my wrist and pondering how many thousands of miles we were away from the nearest BUPA hospital.

I was nervous of getting back on top of this death trap, but Jack pointed out that it would be far quicker to get back to safety (and a restorative G & T) on the cart than on foot, so I reluctantly clambered aboard again, with all the enthusiasm of someone reboarding the *Titanic*. You can imagine my response, when we finally got back into the crew's orbit, to the director's comment, 'Oh, we wondered where you'd got to. We thought that you had decided to do a runner and head back to the hotel without us!' Cue laughter from the crew, short-lived once we told them what had actually happened. They were deeply concerned about my health, having long identified me as the key talent on this particular operation.

Two scans later, some heavy-duty strapping and eight sessions of physio back in London, and I was as good as new (although some family members have suggested that 'new' is a bit of an overstatement). Not that I got any sympathy from my son, who instead thought it amusing to point out that I'd had four weeks away from Mrs Whitehall and came back with a strained wrist. A cheap joke even by his extremely low standards.

I think it's very unlikely that I would have joked about such a thing. I remember giving him nothing but sympathy. And by 'him' I mean the horse, the real victim of this poor story. He's probably in a lasagne now.

A message from our producers: No animals were hurt in the making of this anecdote.

Rental Cars

Many families will fork out on a rental car. But be warned, despite the freedom this may afford you, it's usually outweighed by the hassle. It's like travelling around in a Fabergé egg. The whole holiday becomes about not damaging the bloody car, as if that's inevitably going to happen. Which seems strange, because we use the one at home all the time, and the last time I looked it wasn't crumpled in a heap like something out of *GTA*. If parents could, they would have all the children bound and entombed in bubble wrap before entering the rental car for their own peace of mind. The family could be dragged from a rental car by armed bandits, thrown onto it, beaten up against the windscreen, robbed and left for dead. When you finally came round, the first question a parent would ask would not be: 'Is everyone OK?' It would be: 'Oh my God, did the paintwork get scratched when our son's head hit the bonnet?'

Also, while we are on the subject, why are car rental offices always a bus journey from any airport arrivals terminal? I guess it's to sell you even harder on the idea of getting a car by reminding you of the added misery of any other form of transport. The art of dragging the luggage on to a crowded shuttle bus and then along a 200-yard path to the office is one that has to be perfected over many years. Of course, early on in your adult life you may have the added training aids of a screaming (possibly in my case drugged-up) toddler in a buggy and a baby strapped to your chest in a sling. At least you can console yourself with the knowledge that it won't be too long before said toddler and baby will be old enough to help you with this task. You may be cursing their existence

now, but what you've gestated is a future workforce. Maybe that romantic night in with a bottle of wine wasn't such a bad idea after all. What you will then come to learn is that there is a short window where you can get them to help mule the bags, usually by lying to them that it's some sort of game, before they lurch into the teenage years and you will only get help from them when the request is accompanied with the offer of a bribe, invariably financial as the barter system won't cut it. I can still remember being a teenager, and operating this extortion racket with all the skill of a Kray twin. Still, you will quickly realise that it's a small price to pay to avoid starting every holiday with a slipped disc.

Things seldom get any better when you finally reach the nirvana of the (hopefully) air-conditioned car rental office. Or as I always think of it, the carpet-tiled graveyard of all your best-laid plans. The words any parent dreads more than any other at the desk are: 'Good news. We don't have any cars left in "small category" that you requested. But we have given you upgrade to bigger car, for same price.'

'But I don't want a bigger car; I want the Fiat Punto that I ordered,' says my mother in desperation.

'But we are giving you BMW,' says the bemused car rental clerk, who is confused as to why these red-faced Brits are not looking elated at the prospect of being the beneficiaries of his largesse and thanking him as a veritable Santa Claus of this tarmac Lapland.

'Do you know the cost of refilling a BMW?' barks my father. 'I want the Punto!'

'We only have BMW. No other cars!' persists the clerk.

There then ensues an hour-long conversation about insurance, the clerk doing his very best to sell my parents

additional cover and them acting like this is all some Bernie Madoff-style scam to steal their life savings, resorting to getting the calculator up on their phones (this in itself adds twenty minutes), working out the different excesses on offer, cross-referencing with their policies back home, checking other providers on the internet, thereby eventually wearing down the once charming but now stroppy clerk into submission before exiting the office with no extras purchased. Although given the neurotic fear of accidental damage that overshadows the rest of the holiday, you might wonder if they should have paid for some additional cover and been a little less Dom Littlewood about the whole thing.

And then there's the horror of seeing the drug dealer's car that has been foisted on them against their will. It is not only electric blue, but also has diamond-cut wheel trims. This little detail will mean at least an additional half an hour will need to be factored in to all future journeys, because my father will need to leap out at every parking space and guide my mother into it with laser precision, such is the fear of getting even the tiniest of nicks on those diamond-cut wheel trims (although you would think that if it takes something as hard as a diamond to cut the sodding things, they're probably capable of looking after themselves), as this would result in a £500 charge on the credit card the car company had insisted on swiping before we were allowed to leave the building.

'Why are all the kerbs abroad so high and unforgiving?' my mother grumbles, as she edges the BMW back and forth and back and forth under my father's gimlet eye. Ideally, they'd be leaving this car overnight not in a parking space, but in a crushed velvet box.

And every time we spotted one of the cars that we had reserved, my father would gesticulate at the unsuspecting tourists driving it and shout, 'I bet that's our bloody Punto!'

Road Trip

Of course, some people will bypass the plane, car rental and train altogether and opt instead to drive their own car all the way. Whatever money you may save by choosing this option, it is a false economy. Whatever financial belt tightening can be done to avoid this should be done – shortening the trip, leaving behind a family member, downgrading the villa, sleeping under a tarpaulin in a field if you have to. Do anything you can so you don't have to endure the hellish day-long car journey to get to your destination.

I still have nightmares about the mammoth drives to Cornwall or the Lake District, like *Apocalypse Now* with more Radio 4.

Trapped in a hot, leather-upholstered Volvo estate, the windows steaming up, clasping a plastic carrier bag in case I or any of my siblings threw up, as the wet dog in the back leaps around, moulting all over the luggage.

The worst element of any long car journey with my mother is having to listen to *The Archers* crackling in and out of reception on the radio. It's such a distinctive part of this personal hell on a motorway for me, that to this day when I hear *The Archers* theme tune it makes my stomach churn and I can genuinely smell that heady mixture of gut acid and Werther's Original. My mother is an *Archers* fanatic, an Ambridge Addict. This particular vice meant no car journey was ever undertaken without the accompaniment of *The*

Archers omnibus, a diabolical compendium of the week's tedious serial. All six episodes. That's over an hour of people sitting in a radio studio talking about farming and repeatedly pretending to open doors and pour tea. Even before the advent of the BBC catch-up service or the podcast, my mother would religiously 'record' these elongated editions onto cassette tapes, both sides, so as not to miss any nuggets of rural wisdom from the cast, who, confusingly, all sounded exactly the same. I don't know what's happened to those tapes now, but I wouldn't be surprised if they'd been used by the CIA to break the spirit of political prisoners.

'Can we at least stop off at McDonald's for lunch?' we'd beg my parents in the hope that we might get twenty minutes' respite from Eddie Grundy's latest scrumpy dilemma or Ruth Archer bleating on about a gassy cow! How do I still know all their fucking names?! They are my shoe bombers.

'No need for fast food, children; I've made us all a picnic,' she would say with all the jollity of the truly unhinged. No Happy Meal for us; instead, a Tupperware of car-warmed Scotch eggs and a communal bottle of back-washed Diet Coke, aka the Misery Meal. And she had the temerity to call it a picnic, talk about breadcrumbing a turd. Picnic makes it sound glamorous. Let's face it, Mother, it was rations for those imprisoned against their will. And what kind of monster brings eggs into a boiling car? It was so hot in there I'm surprised none of them hatched!

And so begins the crescendoing choruses of 'are we there yet?' from the back (even though we'd only been on the road for twenty minutes), as my father flails around with an AA route map so old that it doesn't feature Milton Keynes, all because the Sat-Nav had been hurled out of the window in a

fit of road rage at the first roundabout possibly because he's uncomfortable taking orders from a woman's voice. The utter farce of getting lost and your father resolutely refusing to ask for directions, as he deems it 'emasculating'. You're in the middle of rural France, with night drawing in, you've been driving around in circles for hours and the only sustenance we have is Mummy's 'picnic'.

'Please, Daddy, for the love of God, ask one of these farmers for directions.'

'There's no point in asking them for directions, they're all foreign.'

Don't ask them for directions because they are all foreign? We are in a foreign country! Their country! Please tell me you can see the flaw in that logic.

Whining and Dining

Eating Out

YOU SHOULD TRY EVERYTHING once, except haggis and cod sperm. That's the gastronomic equivalent of the old incest and morris dancing idiom. And it is one by which the intrepid traveller should live, delving into the local cuisine whenever possible and broadening horizons – and your waistline – in the process. Why, then, does eating out abroad so often end in bankruptcy or indigestion? The list of pitfalls is long and includes anything from a three-hour ethical debate about how much you should tip, to an experiment with the Gambas Pil Pil that leaves you having to down a herd's worth of milk and sweating from areas of your body you didn't even know had pores. Eating out abroad is a voyage of discovery, but it's sometimes the discovery of just how long you can find yourself staring at the back of a toilet door.

The sober truth is that just being in the country in which a dish originated is no safeguard from disappointment. It's a sad day when you realise that having travelled all the way to China, they don't know what you're talking about when you ask for sesame prawn toasts. That the Indian in India isn't quite up to the standards of the tikka masala from the Star of Bombay on Putney High Street. And they don't even have Nando's in Portugal. What the piri piri fuck?! No wonder Mr Nando had to emigrate, carrying with him just a spicy sauce, a headful of dreams and a disdain for the concept of waited tables.

Sure, every family starts the holiday with the best intentions – to walk the path less trodden – but deep down we all know it's just a case of seeing how long it will take us to break and find the only place on the Amalfi coast that serves a full English breakfast. Don't beat yourself up about it. As you tuck into your eggs and bacon in the sweltering sunshine, feel no shame. Even if around you everyone's toes are curling in their Gucci loafers, thinking, 'Thank God these people Brexited, it's time to put mines down the centre of the Channel and change the locks.' Look, if you want to eat black pudding in a UNESCO World Heritage site that is your prerogative! Three cheers for cosmopolitanism. It's a two-way street.

There's nothing worse than spending the whole holiday fantasising about a mythical culinary experience, seeking out that restaurant that 'only the locals know about'.

'Trust me,' my mother will gloat, 'the nice man from the cheese stall in the market told me only local townsfolk go there. It will be magical.'

If only the locals know about it, why on earth would they

have told us? They've kept it to themselves for all these years but suddenly a loud, dysfunctional English family arrives and they think, 'These guys are special; we must show them to Narnia. We'd always restricted our clientele as part of a deliberate attempt to stagnate our business and make as little money as possible, but completely out of the blue, we've decided that that all changes tonight!' Reality-check, woman!

Besides, there tends to be a very good reason this restaurant is not on TripAdvisor: it's very rustic, it doesn't even have a card machine, it only has one item on the menu and is only open for an hour a day. Right, Mother, are you sure this is a restaurant and not just someone's house? It sounds like the 'nice man from the cheese stall' has invited you over to his bedsit for dinner. That one item on the menu – would it happen to have some sort of dairy component? You're not being told about a secret restaurant; you're being groomed by a cheesemonger.

Even if it turns out not to be a trail of Stilton to his bedroom and a genuine eating establishment, it is never going to be as good as you think, as you have made the fatal error now of overhyping it. At the end of the day, it will just be a restaurant. You can be sure that having made the trek for three days through treacherous mountains, crossed an elderly gypsy lady's palm with silver to find the secret path and signed the non-disclosure agreement before entering, you'll take one look at the menu and decide you fancy the burger. We are, as I say, creatures of habit.

The problem is people are too desperate to do what they think they should be doing on holiday – 'chasing the authentic' – rather than giving in to their baser urges and just following their belly.

All credit to my mother, she can't be accused of betraying her principles. She'll stick to local cuisine, even when the locals themselves don't. Even when they've spent hundreds of years striving to avoid it. We went on holiday to Ukraine and she ate borscht every night for a week. 'I just feel that I should eat like a local.'

Not only did this heavily beetroot-based diet result in her thinking she had developed a UTI every time she went to the bathroom, but she also in all honesty seemed to be having a pretty torrid time when the borscht was entering her system too. Glumly shovelling in forkfuls of stuff that looked as though it had leaked out of a Chernobyl outflow pipe. There's a reason Ukrainian food isn't more celebrated around the world; there was a London-themed steak house next to the hotel, for God's sake. If you find British-themed eateries, you know you're in a country with extremely low standards. Being abroad and seeing a British restaurant is like being in Britain and seeing a Frankie & Benny's – you know it's what people have settled for because the alternatives are even worse. I doubt there are many British-themed restaurants in a culinary powerhouse like Paris. A Manchester Grill on the Champs-Élysées or beg, borrow or steal a reservation at Montmartre's Le Kebab du Newcastle. Look, if you're in France, yes, maybe stick to the bouilla-baisse, but let's face it: some countries' food isn't much to write home about.

Germany is a wonderful nation with an incredible foot-ball team and a thriving economy, the nation that gave us Beethoven and Brecht (yes, they also gave us one of the greatest evils ever to face humanity, but I've already covered diamond-cut wheel trims). However, their cuisine is – to put

it diplomatically – challenging. No one in their right mind wants a diet that is that sausage-heavy, not even the greatest lover of innuendo. Germans will literally stick a sausage in anything (careful). That's why they kept trying to take over the world: it wasn't *Lebensraum*; it was a desperate quest for sausageless cuisine before the entire nation collapsed and died of scurvy.

'What's your favourite?' is my mother's other classic question to ask the waiter when dining out abroad. Nice work, Mother, shall we borrow his pen and write 'MUG' on our foreheads while we are at it? Their favourite is whatever the chef has a load of, sitting around the kitchen gathering mould. Don't believe them when they say that's a crust on the top of the parmesan, it's probably penicillin. Whatever the waiter says is his 'favourite' is the one dish you want to avoid like the plague. Unless you want the next three days with its symptoms. Be wary of descriptions like 'aged beef' or 'heritage cauliflower' – why on earth would I want an old cauliflower? I want fresh cauliflower, vibrant, modern legumes, not ones that have been sat in the pantry for generations.

'Sun-dried squid! That sounds exotic. I'll have that.'

I bet that was just squid when it went on to the menu, Mother. That 'sun-dried' has been scribbled on with a Sharpie because nobody ordered it. It's not part of the recipe, just the effects of the passing of time. That is a pivot from the kitchen if ever I saw one. They've clearly seen you coming a mile off. They went with 'sun-dried' because 'rapidly decomposing' sounded mildly less appetising. But she won't listen to me, so we have to have the rest of the meal with Mother resolutely refusing to admit she's been stitched up, chewing through something that has the consistency of a burnt-out

tyre. Instead of eating it, she might as well stretch it out and use it to fire croutons across the table like a catapult.

Steer clear of waiters' 'recommendations' – and of squid in general, for that matter. For 'squid ink risotto' is another holiday favourite. My mum loves ordering that, a dish that should not be consumed in public unless you've brought your toothbrush out with you. Unless your main aim is to convince the local population that the reputation of British dentistry is not ill-deserved. Squid ink is a staple ingredient in recipes for embarrassment. Just try it someday: wandering around the old town with your mother flashing her blue-black grin at strangers, who swiftly pull away their children because she looks like a crackhead. It's even worse when she goes up to them and tells them she knows a place they can go if they 'want a taste of something very special'.

Another 'exotic-sounding' dish she once ordered for my father when we were in France was an *andouillette saucisse*.

'You like sausages, Michael.'

The problem was that this *saucisse* had nothing to do with what my father recognised to be a sausage. It was the kind of thing you'd order someone who was dangerously addicted to sausages, to act as a form of aversion therapy. It was a dark glistening behemoth that looked more like something that belonged in the window display of a sex shop, made of lumps of chitterlings, a sweet-sounding word but actually that's pig intestines to the uninitiated . . . And that's how they get you. Give it a fancy French name and no one's going to suspect foul play. Just like the difference between the mysterious, enigmatic French 'ménage à trois' and the arguably less poetic, possibly more down-to-earth, English 'spit roast'.

When his *saucisse* arrived, Michael was very dismayed. 'I thought it was going to be like a British banger!'

Don't be so precious. Also, what does he think goes into a British banger? It ain't the fillet, Mike; that's ear and arseholes all day long. Now, come on, lube it up with some Châteauneuf-du-Pape and get it down you.

'You can have anything, children, except the steak,' my father will bark in most restaurants. For him, eating out abroad is all about preventing the natives from feasting on his traveller's cheques, exacerbated by the fact that he's got a sparrow's appetite himself and is as tight as a nun's fanny (I'm not referring to a nun's elasticated luggage pouch here, but her actual fanny).

'But I'm hungry, Daddy.'

'Then stuff up on the bread; this place is a clip joint!'

'You chose it! We would have been happy with Burger King! Why have you picked a restaurant just so you can complain?'

For a man so hell-bent on getting his value for money, it's a surprise how much he changes his tune at the end of the meal, when my mother, noticing that we have been forced to consume far too much complimentary bread and consequently left all of our main courses, starts eyeing up the plates with her 'doggy bag' eyes.

'Please, Hilary, not here. Just let them take the plates away.'

'And let all this good food go to waste? There are children starving all over the world, Michael.'

'There are children starving here, Mother, as I wasn't allowed the steak.'

'Shh, Jack. You've had more than enough bread. You children went at those ciabattas like seagulls.'

'Just let me ask the waiter to bag it up for me. You never know, you might get hungry later.'

'I think, if I do by some miracle feel hungry later, I will not be in the mood for your leftover risotto. By the way, you should probably have some mouthwash before we get in the taxi, or the driver will think we're taking you to score.'

But there's no way of getting through to her. And so the taxi ride back to the hotel will be spent trying not to heave as I nurse a lapful of warm tortellini in a napkin and a sanitary bag of crab claws.

'I'll take those back and whip them up into a bisque.'

'How, Mother? We're staying in a hotel.'

'The kettle?'

Good luck! It's already tucked away in my hand luggage.

She needed to take a roll of bin liners with her to doggy-bag up the amount of food we had left over in the restaurants on a trip to America.

You must always remember that the portion they give you in a US diner is for a week, not a single sitting. I think it's for historical reasons – they give you just about the amount of food you'd need to survive the entire voyage of the *Mayflower*.

America is truly the bellybutton of the obesity epidemic, and it's an outy. The sheer scale of the excesses is breathtaking. Even though breathtaking is one of the many things you will find increasingly difficult if you eat out there a lot. It's like no one has ever heard of portion control, or what constitutes a 'side'. Beef brisket mac 'n' cheese is a main meal! One meal! In most British restaurants, that's half the whole menu. And don't get me started on the 'side of pancakes'!

If your side dish is literally a plate stacked so high that you can't see over it, then it's not a side: you've just ordered two breakfasts. It's a privacy screen of carbohydrates.

They are brazen about it too. I visited one restaurant where you could order a Bypass Burger. To be fair, the restaurant in question, which was in Vegas – where else?! – was called the 'Heart Attack Grill', so I guess you wouldn't opt for a table there if you were looking for restraint. I don't know how they came up with the name, presumably the Chronic Obstructive Pulmonary Disease Bistro seemed, ironically, too much of a mouthful. This was a restaurant where you're served by ladies in nurse outfits and can be wheeled out on a stretcher if you eat too much. It's literally the kind of place that makes you think we may have failed as a civilisation. Still, it's probably the only restaurant in the world whose clientele has a higher average blood pressure than the diners at Daddy's club, the Garrick.

The free refill is a hard concept for us Brits to get our heads round as well, so brought up are we to seize any opportunity to get anything on the house, believing that there will surely only be minutes before it's taken away by the police or perhaps the Conservative Party. Once we realise that the coffee is unlimited, we feel obliged to drink them dry and get our money's worth, with scant regard for the fact that with that much caffeine in the system we won't sleep for days. There may be no such thing as a free lunch, but there certainly is such a thing as an espresso-induced anxiety meltdown. As if the metric gallon of coffee weren't enough to get us on edge, the Brit vacationing Stateside also has to navigate the utterly foreign concept of 'customer service'. We have clear expectations of customer service in the UK. What we

expect is that when we eventually pay the bill, the person holding the card machine will at some point mutter the word 'cheers'. Anything else is a totally unlooked-for bonus. Having someone smile at you and ask you if you're 'enjoying your meal' after practically every mouthful is a concept so alien to Europeans, we don't know how to respond, so used are we to waiters treating us with apathy or contempt. The American server, therefore, is a disconcerting species. The whole thing triggers our fight or flight response.

'Is this man trying to fuck me? He keeps grinning and asking me how my day has been. How do I make it stop?'

'I think he's just being nice, Daddy.'

'Angling for a big tip, eh? I know your game, sunshine. I'm not that easy.'

'You're playing hard to get, Daddy. Now who's flirting with whom?'

The fatal error my family makes on every holiday is to eat cheap and cheerful for most of the fortnight, and then have a blowout on one fancy meal towards the end. Heaping all the pressure on to one night can only end badly. Besides, taking my family to anything approaching 'haute cuisine' is like taking a pig to the opera. Fine dining *en famille* is a hard no, especially with my gastronomically blinkered family. My siblings' palates are probably sufficiently stimulated by a bucket of Kentucky Fried Chicken, and if one of us ate the lemon wipe by mistake we probably wouldn't notice. When fine dining, we're an absolute liability. And while the British culture of not really having customer service is, for the most part, quite comforting, there is a limit to how rude staff in a restaurant can be to you. And some fancy restaurants, especially on the Continent, can take la pisse.

Everything is stacked against you in those places. Even the menu. Now this is an unpopular opinion, but I think the more expensive the restaurant, the more willing they should be to have pictures of the food. It's always dodgy roadside kebab shops that have pictures of their food. Why?! What are they telling us – 'this guy knows how to handle a camera, so he can probably handle a microwave'? For a start, it always looks grim and nothing you would want to advertise. Also, we all know what a burger looks like and even if it isn't as you expected, and they cock it up, put the bread in the middle and the patties on the outside, you've only wasted a couple of quid. You'll survive.

In nice restaurants, though, you're spending a fortune on the dish and the stakes, excuse the pun, are considerably higher, so you at least want to know what you're getting. If Daddy had seen a picture of that andouillette, he'd have known not to order it (to be honest, the sight of it would probably have put him off ordering anything at all and giving serious consideration to giving up eating altogether). But not only do they not have pictures in fancy restaurants, there is now a trend to be incredibly vague and cryptic on the menus as well. Instead of a description of the dish you are paying a fortune for, you get a riddle.

I went with my family to a Michelin-starred restaurant, I won't reveal in which country, but I picked up the menu and the first starter listed was *Oeuf*. OK, it was France.

'Egg.' That's what the dish was called: 'Egg'. I'm going to need a bit more than that before forking out thirty quid on it. I've eaten in French restaurants, I know that pretty much anything can turn out to be a sausage made of anuses. And here we're dealing with the egg, famously one of the most

versatile of foods, a veritable shapeshifter that can be cooked practically any way possible.

We looked closer. Beneath, in italics, it read: 'Two eggs, one farm, three textures.' Who wrote this menu? Dr Seuss? My father called over the snooty waitress and asked for some more details.

'The descriptions are ambiguous so the diner can go on a journey,' she explained.

'I'm fine with a journey, darling,' he replied, perhaps a little too forcibly, 'I just want to know the destination.'

I guess he had a point. If you were going on a train you wouldn't go to the ticket booth, hand over three hundred quid and just say, 'Surprise me.'

And I'm not one of those people that likes to ask endless questions about the food. Nor do I want that much information. I couldn't give a toss where my chicken came from, what its name was, where it went to school and all that nonsense. I don't want my chicken to have a past. I want it to be a mysterious enigma, a beautiful stranger. Especially as they are always so desperate to tell you how brilliant a life it had, running around fields and picking daisies, while having Shakespeare read to it by an artisanal farmhand, before it had its head chopped off, feathers plucked and was flattened with a brick so I could eat it. It always makes it sound as if you've snuffed out the life of what could have been the chicken Malala for your tikka masala. If anything, they should tell you how terrible a life the chicken had.

'The chicken you're eating tonight, sir, couldn't wait for it all to end. Why did it cross the road? Because it was suicidal. It threw itself in front of a car. All its chicken relatives were just thankful its long ordeal was over. So don't feel any

guilt at all you gifted it the sweet release of death. Side of spring greens?'

All I need to know is what I'm ordering. But in the case of 'Egg', I decided to take a punt. If for no other reason than it might wind up my dad. 'Egg' arrived and it was, as with all things gastronomical, utterly preposterous.

Two eggs, some stuff smeared underneath one of them, and both of them covered in foam. I could see instantly why they were so coy in the first place. It looked like two poached eggs with a case of rabies. Which would have been a much clearer description for the menu; I wouldn't order it but at least I'd know what my 'destination' was.

While 'Egg' got my father bristling, it wasn't until dessert that we encountered the straw that broke the camel's back. My father has simple tastes when it comes to pudding. As a result, he ordered the deceptively straightforward 'Strawberry' and, no exaggeration, waited patiently for thirty minutes. My mother, as she always does in these situations, was trying to calm him down. Really the best way of dealing with Daddy is to treat him like a crisis that simply has to be calmly managed.

'It's fine, Michael, just relax, we're on holiday, don't make a scene. It's not like we have a plane to catch.'

'We have tomorrow morning and the speed with which they are making this "Strawberry", we'll be missing it!' I don't know what he imagined was going on in the kitchen, perhaps a load of people in chef's whites waiting around a strawberry plant on the off chance something might germinate. He couldn't and wouldn't let it go. He beckoned over the waitress and, to give him credit, in what was by his standards a very calm tone asked, 'Do you have any idea why my dessert is taking so long to make?'

You could have a team of scriptwriters work for a month and not come up with a response so laser-guided to enrage him. It was the sort of remark that wouldn't be possible without thousands of years of French history, most of it spent thinking of ways to effectively wind up the English.

The waitress rolled her eyes and said, 'Because the chef is not making a dessert, he is making art.'

'Oh, why didn't you say? Well, maybe you could pop back there and get him off his potter's wheel and ask him to start making my crème brûlée or mille-feuille or whatever the fuck *Strawberry* is!' I was worried he might start foaming at the mouth, and we'd already had more than enough of that with 'Egg'.

He's making art. Really? It was one of those rare occasions where I was kind of on my father's page just a teeny bit. It was quite cathartic to watch him go ballistic!

'Do you know what's going to happen to his art? I'm going to put it in my mouth and in six hours' time, it will have turned into a poo. Maybe someone could go into his kitchen – or studio, he probably calls it a studio – and remind him of that. I reckon Picasso might have rattled out *Guernica* a bit quicker if he knew that a day after finishing it, it was going to be flushed down a lavatory!'

Thankfully, by this point the waitress had long since left, probably to the kitchen to encourage the entire staff of the restaurant to add a few extra bodily fluids to the long-awaited Strawberry.

Eventually father calmed down and I pointed out to him that the real baller move would be to wait until they gave him the astronomical bill and when they asked him to sign his name just put 'Man'.

'Sir, we are going to need more detail.'

Tell them you like to keep your identity ambiguous so that their accounts department can go on a journey.

We haven't been back to a Michelin-starred restaurant on holiday since. Far safer to stick to room service! You don't have such a rich experience, but at least Daddy and the outside world don't have to meet each other.

It's not just fine dining that can cause a meltdown of nuclear proportions. I wanted to tell this next story but wasn't trusted to, as the last time I did, apparently I took quite a lot of 'liberties' and left out some vital details. So I'll give Daddy the chance to reveal it to you in his own words. I warn you, once you have read this you will never be able to look at him the same way again . . .

Michael: CHERNOBYL

My Achilles heel has always been my stomach. It is a delicate flower; a little less so now, since a gifted surgeon called Mr Menzies-Gow performed some nifty surgery in my fifties. I don't know the ins and outs, but the poor doctor looked as though he'd been through an ordeal afterwards and sported something of a thousand-yard stare. He did, in fact, give me a DVD of the procedure upon discharging me from hospital, but it's hard to know if there's ever the right time to suggest watching that of an evening.

'Children, come downstairs please! Your mother and I are doing a screening.'

Still, thanks to Mr Menzies-Gow's wizardry, my stomach has been in much better order, but it still has a habit of

wrong-footing me on the odd occasion. In one particularly dramatic case, it struck in the most inconvenient of places.

I could not have picked a more extreme location than Chernobyl, the most toxic environment on earth. To be fair, there is an e-waste facility in Agbogbloshie in Ghana that claims to be more toxic, and I certainly don't want to get bogged down in any dispute over local bragging rights. So, to be strictly accurate, Chernobyl is one of the most toxic places on the planet. I'm pretty sure that the people who compile these lists never visited Jack's halls of residence in Manchester, as that might have relegated both of the above.

I never quite understood Jack's fascination with going to Chernobyl. I got his desire for us to participate in the International Clown Festival in Odessa. That was an experience of a lifetime, not to mention a great chance for Jack to see what his future in children's entertainment might look like once the TV work has inevitably dried up post my retirement. I even bought into the idea of visiting Australia, despite my fondness for cool climates and culture! But Chernobyl? The site of the most cataclysmic nuclear accident in history? Why? There was nothing doing: Jack was determined that we should go and check it out. I have been pleasantly surprised before. The killing caves in Cambodia were not as grim as I had anticipated, and in some ways made for quite an informative afternoon. Even Las Vegas wasn't quite as ghastly as I'd imagined.

Our diligent producers spent months getting it all sorted out. Given their track record – including the booking of our disastrous Romanian cart-ride – I was keen they should properly organise the piss-up in this particular brewery. As you can imagine, you can't rock up unannounced at the gates of

the Exclusion Zone, full film crew in tow, and expect just to be waved in to film at will. No, this trip required months of form-filling, emails back and forth with the authorities in Ukraine, detailed profiles on the pared-down crew, documents listing exactly what we were and weren't allowed to film, and a minute-by-minute schedule of how the whole day would play out. Clearly, the Ukrainians had learnt a harsh lesson from what had befallen them. Although these precautions did feel a bit like shutting the stable door after the nuclear reactor had exploded.

I had mentioned on several occasions that, perhaps, this Chernobyl endeavour might be somewhat light on comedy, but I was ready to accept that, sometimes, in order to help the comedy punch through, you need a more serious subject in juxtaposition to the laughs. In much the same way that Jack generally acts as the downbeat blank canvas against which my bons mots sparkle. As it happened, it was to be me that provided the farce that particular day.

The visit started well. We sailed through the many ruthless security checks, passed the repeated body scans and, as far as I can tell, failed to make the whole situation there any worse than it already was. It was as we approached our lunch break in the Chernobyl staff canteen, which although a break, was to be filmed, that things began to unravel for me.

I should start by saying that the producers had told me the previous evening that the weather was going to be extremely cold, so perhaps I might wish to layer up for the day's filming. I therefore had not just a full set of thermal underwear under my signature tweed three-piece suit, and of course a tie, but I was also attired in woollen socks, fur-lined boots, a heavy wool overcoat and all finished off

with a scarf, gloves and hat. I suspect that unconsciously I was trying to give the gamma rays as many obstacles to pass through as possible. As it turned out, it was a glorious and actually quite balmy sunny day, so layers needed to be ditched as early as possible. Unfortunately, this was not practicable until just before lunch, so I was forced to struggle through the morning's filming with the heat (which I hope came from the sun rather than anything more sinister). Jack suggested I remain in the crew minibus and divest myself of my thermal undergarments, while they went in to recce the canteen. This proved to be quite tricky, given the space constraints in the minibus (not to mention the abundant windows, which meant I risked creating a spectacle almost as awe-inspiring as the reactor itself).

It might be useful at this point if I ran through the very strict protocols that we were instructed to adhere to while we were on site. We were to follow our guide's instructions at all times: wash our hands when required. No food or drinks could be brought on site and we were only to eat and drink when in the canteen. The existence of all these rules and regulations is just one of the many reasons why, to my mind, Chernobyl is unlikely any time soon to rival the likes of Legoland as a holiday-making destination. No animals were to be stroked or touched, as if I needed to be warned of that. And we were to stick to the designated routes and paths through the entire facility, and nothing was to touch the ground. This was imperative, as there are still many hotspots of contamination all over the zone. Hence my being banished to the minibus.

By the time I had finished my partial de-robing, I was even hotter than when I started and certainly quite bothered. Still,

there were the eagerly anticipated delights of the Chernobyl canteen to spur me on. All this activity had made me quite peckish, and there really is nothing like the sight of history's worst man-made disaster to help you work up an appetite.

The first thing that happened on arrival inside was that we were overrun by a stag party – from Barnsley! I guess, given that they were about to visit the town of Pripyat, an eerie wasteland suspended in the year 1986, at least having come from Barnsley, it would have been far less shocking. Nevertheless, a stag party did seem out of place in Chernobyl, where the sight of a man wearing a pair of plastic breasts would be taken less as a humorous novelty, more a sign of a tragic, nuclear-triggered mutation.

We managed to avoid this rowdy group by heading straight to the servery, where we were confronted by a line of ladies in pristine white catering uniforms, which included an impressive display of chef's hats. They stood behind a small array of lunch choices.

'What is this, please?' I asked one of them, pointing to some unidentifiable slices of what looked like rather insipid ham.

'Meat.'

'May I ask what type of meat?' I enquired further.

'Mixed meat,' she elaborated. It seemed the distressing fad of ambiguous descriptions of food had even reached Chernobyl.

As there didn't appear to be any other choices, apart from something that may have been the fish-based option, and which looked suspiciously like it had two heads, I plumped for 'mixed meat'. This was served with some grated carrot and a couple of spoonfuls of heavily beetroot-based salads.

The drinks situation was, at best, limited. Not a sommelier in sight. There was, however, a tray of glasses filled with a pale coloured liquid with lumps floating in it. I assumed that it had been dredged from whatever served as the habitat of the two-headed fish.

'What is this, please?' I asked the lady manning the drinks counter.

'Fruit drink.'

'Do you have any plain water?' I endeavoured.

'No water. Fruit drink.'

'I think I'll pass on that, thank you,' I muttered under my breath to Jack.

'You better have something to drink, Daddy, it's hot outside.'

'I am not drinking that. It looks like it's come out of the bottom of the dishwasher! I sort of expected that there might be a vodka option, given where we are.'

'We're in the middle of Chernobyl, Daddy, where there are hundreds of people decommissioning nuclear reactors, so I don't think vodka at lunchtime is the best idea!' He had a point, given that sort of thing may well have been the cause of the whole disaster in the first place. I'm the last person to pipe up in favour of health and safety, but if it stopped people from splitting the atom while hammered, that much is probably no bad thing.

As I have specified earlier, Jack and I taking lunch in the Chernobyl canteen was to make up some of the filmed sequence. Only as we sat down at the communal table with the camera crew did it fully dawn on me that I was actually going to have to eat some of this stuff. I've long argued that a stuntman should be used to cover some of the more

unappealing parts of programme-making – long walks, staircase-climbing, listening to Jack's anecdotes – but thus far without success, possibly because of a shortage of eighty-year-old stuntmen.

'Just make sure you don't wolf too much of it down, Daddy,' Jack said helpfully. Very funny.

'No danger of that,' I replied. 'Not with my stomach!'

But as is so often the case when you're filming, you get caught up in the moment and distracted by the narrative that you are delivering, and before I knew it, I had managed to eat well over half of the 'mixed meat'. Just like the tiddly men who once ran the power station, I realised too late that I had made a serious error and the first of what would develop into my very own series of unfortunate events.

Lunchtime over, we left the canteen, and as we drove off in the minibus to our next location, I began to feel the urgent need of a bathroom. A quick request to our local fixer and we made a mini detour to the nearest facilities. It was as I entered the stall to be confronted by two footprints painted on the floor, next to a hole in the ground, with a roll of shiny toilet paper the like of which I hadn't seen since the 1940s, that I quickly realised I should have availed myself of the loo back at the canteen. And that if this had been the level of attention generally paid towards organising the facilities at Chernobyl, then it certainly explained a lot about past events. But we had a strict schedule to adhere to, so there was nothing for it, I was just going to have to shit or get off the figurative pot. I opted to just hold it in. Second serious error.

Twenty minutes later, my stomach decided that it was certainly not holding on to anything, let alone half a plate of

'mixed meat', and as we were being waved through a small checkpoint manned by a solitary official, I realised that what I needed was now a matter of some urgency. Presumably if anywhere was geared up to handle an unexpected crisis, Chernobyl would be.

'I need the loo,' I said as calmly as I could.

'Sorry, Michael,' answered our guide. 'I'm not sure there is a toilet nearby.'

It was at this point that urgency turned into a desperation that could not be ignored for a minute longer. From the depths of my soul and in a primeval voice that took even me by surprise, I stood up and yelled, 'STOP THIS BUS!'

I don't know where that voice came from, it was like the possessed Regan in *The Exorcist* and emanated from deep within – possibly directly from the pile of mixed meat even then ravaging my colon. The driver slammed on the brakes. I ran to the front of the bus, flung open the door and ran back towards the checkpoint, with the guide shouting in Russian to the official what I assumed were enquiries about a toilet. It may just have been the words, 'Don't shoot.' The official pointed to a small nearby shed.

If I thought that the previous toilet was unusable, it was positively luxurious compared to this one. As I hurled myself inside and dropped my trousers, I was overwhelmed by an odour too noxious to describe and started to faint. Luckily, Jack had followed me into the shed and caught me just before I hit the (possibly contaminated) ground. A slap on the face and I was back with him, as he dragged me out into the open.

'I have to go, Jack,' I told him.

'Right, well, you can't touch anything because of the radiation, so we'll have to be creative here,' he replied. 'Grab my

hands and we will both lean back and you do what you need to do. I'll try not to look,' he added.

There then followed one of the most undignified moments of my life, having to do a dump, while executing a sort of X-rated paso doble with my own son in the middle of over-grown wasteground, with a full camera crew and several Chernobyl personnel averting their eyes. I believe even men who had lived through the horrors of 1986 retired afterwards, feeling that this was one atrocity too many. It was at the critical moment of release that we were joined by an inquisitive and friendly dog: one of the many feral dogs that we had been told categorically *not* to touch. It started to bark and josh around the business end of things, wanting to join in with the second biggest nuclear explosion to hit Chernobyl in thirty years. Fortunately, Jack managed to keep hold of me at the same time as shooing it away, waving an outstretched foot in its general direction. While I am sceptical about many of his so-called talents, his contortions that day convinced me he could certainly do a great job on *Strictly*.

My duty done, I began to feel faint again. The whole experience had taken a lot out of me, both figuratively and literally. Jack called to the crew and a couple of them came running over. It was only as we saw the ashen face of our usually very smiley soundman that I realised that although they were all far enough away not to have witnessed any of these grisly events, we still had our radio mics on and he had heard the full horror of it all in glorious stereo.

Having regained my composure, the guide was insistent that I have immediate medical attention. Despite my pro-testations to the contrary, he called for an ambulance from Chernobyl Hospital (not, I believe, BUPA-accredited). It didn't

take long to appear, and with it a doctor in a white coat along with a late-middle-aged lady in a cardigan, who I assumed was his assistant. It was only when she whipped a stethoscope out from beneath her knitwear and started to examine me, barking orders at her colleague in the white coat, that I realised she was in fact the doctor and he the assistant, contrary to my usual sexist assumptions. I should have remembered that the former USSR was famous for its impressive female role models, like Rosa Klebb in *From Russia with Love* and, of course, all of those Olympic shot-putters.

My cardigan-clad protector was adamant that I needed to be blue-lit back to hospital, so that I could have a proper once-over. I, in turn, insisted that Jack carry on with the filming, so as not to waste the months it had taken to set this up. We would reconvene, I said, back at the hospital once he was finished. So off he went with the crew to Pripyat and off I went with the medics to hospital.

When I say 'blue-lit': the ambulance was circa late 1970s, so it was more of a leisurely trip back to the hospital, itself also circa the 1970s. I don't think anything had changed since they treated all the victims of the disaster. Though I certainly hope they'd wiped down the surfaces. But what I would say is that the care I received that afternoon was exemplary. I had the undivided attention of at least six doctors and, at one stage, a giant, burly hospital security guard (I believe male, but once again one must be very careful about these often clumsy assumptions), who joined in with the battery of tests they ran on me, including a couple of ECGs. I got the impression that they were just thrilled to have a customer to get their hands on. I am not sure how busy they were on a day-to-day basis. They ultimately hooked me up

to a drip because, as they explained to Jack when he eventually arrived, I was severely dehydrated, probably as a result of heatstroke, which had caused my blood pressure to drop. Jack was kind enough to resist saying 'I told you so', as he was just relieved that I was on the mend and that his bizarre obsession with Chernobyl hadn't killed me.

One bag of fluids – which looked suspiciously like the fruit drink from the canteen – later and a promise from me that I would see my own doctor when I got home (inevitable anyway, as we're both members of the Garrick Club), and they were happy to release me. It was at this point, Jack says, that I turned into Prince Charles. I insisted that they all line up in the treatment room so that I could deliver a rousing thank-you speech, simultaneously translated into Russian by our guide, and shake each one of them by the hand, before we headed for the minibus and our long overdue departure.

And the lesson that I took away from this debacle? Annoyingly, my millennial children are right: if it's hot, despite my resistance to it, I definitely need to drink plenty of fluid. Even if it has lumps floating in it. To ensure my physical safety next time we travel abroad to make a programme, I will insist on being accompanied everywhere we go by a full case of Château Latour, on the soundest of medicinal grounds. And if you've read through this and are maybe thinking that Chernobyl could be a fun holiday destination, take my humble advice: swerve the canteen.

International Drinking Rules

In an airport anything goes, so make the most of it. It's like we've decided to declare airports as utterly exempt from the

normal rules of society, a place where laws and liver damage seemingly don't apply. Airports are the only places in the world where you can have a pint in a Wetherspoons at 6 a.m. and people won't look at you thinking, 'There's someone who's made some seriously poor life choices.' No, they think, 'Ooh, they must be going somewhere fun.' So, pull up a stool at the bar, where hopefully they don't know your name, and fill your boots, not literally. Although to be fair, if drinking out of your shoe is your style, Wetherspoons might be just about the only place that kind of behaviour is not frowned upon. Why not go the whole hog and crack open the bubbly, have a champagne breakfast and start your holiday in style? Someone must be buying that bottle of Taittinger behind the bar at Wetherspoons, which always feels to me like the epitome of wishful thinking. Like a Chanel bag hanging above the till at Sports Direct. Or Spurs putting a deposit down for an open-topped bus. Hope over expectation.

Day drinking is, of course, allowed on holiday. Everyone knows that; it is, after all, five o'clock somewhere. Also, if you get stuck into a serious twelve-hour session, then it will have been five o'clock everywhere by the time you've finished. The time difference is the perfect excuse to tuck into a glass of wine before lunch, even if it turns out home is actually a couple of hours behind and you're, therefore, technically, drinking wine for breakfast. It's fine, you're on holiday, and it's rosé after all, which I've always considered a morning tipple. Basically, Ocean Spray with a bit of kick to it.

Be wary of the regional aperitif. A little local tipple can be one of life's great unexpected and more importantly complimentary joys, allowing you to celebrate life the way the locals do – ouzo in Greece, jenever in Belgium, anything

in Scotland. Just make sure you're pissed by the time you drink it, as these tipples tend not to stand up to the sober palate! In Hungary we were offered their local digestif, Unicum, which, incredibly, managed to taste even worse than it sounded. I had to handcuff my father to a beer bike in Heroes' Square in order to get him to even take a sip. Turned out he was a spitter not a swallower of that particular delicacy.

I always try to live by the helpful rhyme, 'Beer then wine, fine. Beer after wine, fine. Wine and more wine also fine. Beer wine beer wine, still fine. Beer then wine then ouzo – fucked.'

Holidays are a great chance to break in the kids, get them ready for the future of alcoholism that they surely have in front of them as a result of having you for parents. Most of my early experiences with the bottle occurred on family holidays. I think my parents to some extent realised the emotional hell they were putting us through and thought it was only reasonable to offer us some form of anaesthetic. I think I was allowed my first egg cup of wine on holiday aged about eight, my first beer around fifteen in France and my first Jägerbomb in Magaluf at eighteen, although to be fair my mum and dad weren't on that particular holiday. Thank fuck. I'm 90 per cent sure they would have ended up in the group that all got tattoos.

And finally, don't be a snob. As you're sat in Spain pickling your liver in sangria, try to enjoy the experience and not be put off by the reality that you're basically drinking a red wine shandy with a bit of fruit floating around in it, a sort of alcoholic version of what was on offer in the Chernobyl canteen. Same goes with beer. Stella Artois back home has

connotations of string vests and flat-roof pubs and things 'kicking off' in a car park, yet for some reason on the Continent it transforms into something far more sophisticated. Sipping it from a frosted demi glass with your shades on like you're in a Fellini film, you're almost tempted to sniff the bouquet. I'm sure any beer decanted into one of those cute little tulip-shaped French beer glasses would look classy.

'Hey, what are you drinking?'

'Le brew du spéciale.'

'Ooh là là, c'est magnifique.'

Exit via the Gift Shop

IT'S IMPORTANT, WHEN GOING abroad, to make sure you give yourself a sensible budget; this is the smart way to avoid cleaning yourself out with any impulsive splurges. Of course, you will have to re-evaluate this budget as soon as you're on the plane, as most of it will have been frittered away on snacks and duty free. Quite why you thought life wouldn't be complete without a 1.75 litre bottle of Disaronno and a tin of shortbread shaped like a London bus will remain a mystery for the rest of the holiday. There's something about seeing alcohol at a reduced price that prompts even the most prudent of us into a fit of recklessness. Still, if you're going to get through the family holiday, being inebriated for most of it is no bad thing.

Being out of pocket is also probably a blessing in disguise as, let's face it, no one has ever bought anything on holiday that they truly come to cherish (with the possible exception

of Imodium). You must know that anything you end up buying abroad will end up collecting dust in a cupboard or on the shelves of a charity shop. The massive ceramic haul from Morocco will not be used once. As soon as you've left Marrakesh and returned to England, your normal diet will resume, a diet which, you seemed to forget at the time, did not include 'tagine Tuesdays'. The tagine dish, therefore, will just take up an exorbitant amount of space in your kitchen and be a constant luminous orange reminder of your lapse in judgement. It may be an authentic product of a cuisine that's endured for more than a millennium, but you'll probably end up keeping your keys in it. Unless you are clever enough to wrap it up and palm it off as an exotic wedding present to the next friend who gets married. The bottle of grappa purchased in Italy will sit unopened for years until one day you have a party, run out of every other spirit and will be unable to find any lighter fluid to drink instead. It is then that you resort to the grappa and, after just one sip, remember why no one outside Italy would touch the stuff. Just imagine what Cicero might have come up with if he'd had access to a Jägerbomb instead. The leather and bead anklet you got on the beach in Barbados will be worn back on the plane, then immediately removed, as being seen in public with it on back home, you would be judged more harshly than if you had an electronic tag around your ankle.

The idea of a souvenir is nice, but surely a memory or a picture is better than a mass-produced piece of plastic shaped like the Eiffel Tower. Even if the kind of memories produced by most family holidays are the sort that therapists spend years helping you to suppress. Worse still is the souvenir with a practical use. My parents' house is littered with such

things, including an oven glove that looks like a pizza from Naples – classy; a backpack with nuclear warning signs on it from Chernobyl – we've found that using it as carry-on luggage tends to create more problems than it solves, although it can earn you a bit of distance on a packed Tube carriage; a peasant's hat made of baby goat skin, which makes my father look like a bloodshot Papa Smurf; and – the *pièce de résistance* – a mug shaped like a pair of lady's boobs, with 'Mykonos' emblazoned across them. I'm not entirely sure what this was supposed to convey about the wonders of the Cyclades. I once saw my granddad drinking hot chocolate out of it. It's a pretty disturbing memory of his head nestled between the ceramic bust, grinning ear to ear with a milk moustache.

My mother also has enough fridge magnets to fill a medium-sized landfill site, a suggestion that has been put to her on more than one occasion. She has so many on the fridge, the weight of them has pulled the door hinges out of alignment. We're getting to the point where there's enough magnetic power in our kitchen, it's starting to be orbited by its own moon.

Haggling

Unfortunately, my mother is aided and abetted by my father, who is even worse. He has always been a magpie for tat. They say a fool and his money are soon parted – especially if said fool is carrying his money around in his wife's fanny pack and has next to no idea how many pounds there are to the peso. He sees something shiny in a market and has to have it. In Istanbul, it was a sword stick.

'I've always wanted one of these, it's very elegant,' he said, slashing it around at head height like a geriatric Zorro, much to my dismay and also to the dismay of the group of market traders who had gathered around, sensing an easy prey for their sales techniques.

'Why? You live in present-day Putney not Victorian Whitechapel,' I said.

'You never know, it might come in handy. It can get quite fiery in the Putney Shopping Exchange come Black Friday.' Quite how a sword stick was going to help him beat a path to the front of the queue in L'Occitane was not immediately clear to me.

'How would you get it back through customs?' I enquired sensibly. Maybe he was thinking of swallowing it.

At this point, the Turkish market trader attempting to peddle the sword stick helpfully chimed in.

'Don't worry, I have many people who purchase these; they get through airport fine. No one ever come back to complain.'

Yes, they probably don't come back to complain because they're rotting in a Turkish jail cell, like John Hurt in *Midnight Express*. You buy that sword stick, the next transaction you'll make will involve a packet of cigarettes and the exchange of protection for sexual favours. Still, there's no reasoning with my father when he decides he wants to buy something; all rational arguments go out the window.

Then comes the moment all children fear. When your father gives you those 'hold my beer' eyes and decides it's time to haggle. Haggling at the best of times is cringe-inducing, and my father will attempt to do it anywhere, even if he's back home in Currys on the high street, trying

to barter down the price of a Scart lead like it's a rug in a Turkish bazaar. He'll try to get money off, ignoring the fact that it's a national chain, with central buying, set prices and he's negotiating not with Mr Curry himself, but a shop assistant who would be fired on the spot if he gave him a discount.

He has even been known to call my mother when she is abroad to purchase something that you can't get in the UK (probably something made out of foie gras or ivory) and insist that when she gets to the moment of paying, she has to FaceTime him, so that he can haggle with the sales assistant 'face to face'.

'I don't suppose you have any discounts going for an old, impoverished English pensioner?' is his usual opener, while feeling in the pocket of his Savile Row suit to ensure his bulging padlocked wallet is safe from attack.

'Sorry, no, sir.'

'Two-for-one offers?'

'No, sir.'

'Discontinued lines or ex-display?'

It's a market stall, Daddy. Everything is ex-display.

It is usually at this point that my mother finally loses the will to live and cuts him off mid-negotiation and starts rummaging for cash in her assortment of fanny packs.

But when Michael is abroad and finally gets his face-to-face haggle, it's even worse. Watching your dad desperately try to get what equates to 50p after the exchange rate off something he didn't even want in the first place is a less than edifying sight. I have seen rats fighting over the remains of a doner kebab that had more dignity. It's worse still in my case, as my father used to be an actors' agent and therefore

prides himself on his skills of negotiation; it's hard-wired into him. It's no longer about the sword stick; it's about his ego, getting his balls out on the table (cobwebbed as they may be) and showing his mettle, flexing the old muscles and proving to his family that he's the Wolf of Wall Street by trying to rip off a man who is probably sleeping in the back of his shop.

'How much for the sword stick?' he will begin.

'One thousand lira,' says the shopkeeper wearily, knowing all too well the dance he's about to go through. This is probably a man whose country has been financially exploited by the English for the best part of the last five hundred years, and he knows it's not going to stop any time soon.

My father laughs.

'Don't be ridiculous, that's far too much . . .' Now, suddenly, an authority on the price of sword sticks. 'How does one hundred sound?'

'It sounds insulting, Daddy,' I chip in helpfully.

'Stay out of this, son, I'm lowballing him. It's a classic negotiation technique.'

'I think five hundred lira sounds a good compromise, Daddy,' I persist. I tend to start worrying about what might happen if things get nasty. I'm always aware at such times that we are in a foreign country, and there are two of us and around eighty million of them.

'Whose side are you on?' he retorts through gritted teeth.

'I'm not on anyone's side, Daddy, I just think five hundred sounds like a very good price for what is, as you say, a very elegant sword stick.'

'I think we might have a wander and come back later. It's just a bit too much for my budget,' my father says through

a shit-eating grin, the sun glinting off his gold Rolex and temporarily blinding the shoeless vendor.

By this point, I already know the play. The next hour will be spent walking round the bazaar – trying and failing to uncover the cut-price sword sticks that Daddy is convinced the locals are keeping from him – knowing full well that we are returning to the trader for a second bite of the cherry.

'Trust me, Jack, always walk away, let them stew on it for an hour or so, start rueing the opportunity missed, then when you do come back, that little Turk will be putty in my hands; watch him roll over.'

'One thousand lira,' says the trader, having seen a thousand tourists try this exact same trick before.

A tense back-and-forth ensues, with the trader finally losing the will to live and deciding to knock it down to 950 and my dad shaking his hand triumphantly. 'Boring the opposition into submission' is not generally thought of as a classic negotiating tactic, but it's one at which my father is an absolute master.

'Well, at least I got a substantial reduction,' says my father, smarting slightly that he couldn't get him to yield more.

'A substantial reduction? You got five quid off, Daddy.'

'What?' says my dad, the colour draining from his face (arguably making him the healthiest he's looked in thirty years).

'Yup, fifty lira is five quid, meaning you got five pounds off and only had to pay him one hundred and eighty pounds.'

You see, what's happened here is that my father has completely miscalculated the exchange rate, assuming, as he always does, that all foreign currency, especially with the name 'lira' attached to it, is essentially Monopoly money. I

knew this all along as I had the conversion rate live-streaming on my mobile phone (what can I say? I'm a fun guy) and, at any point, could have intervened to let him know. But like an *Apprentice* contestant willing their team leader to fail, I just stood back and waited, knowing that I'd eventually get to have my fun in the boardroom. Because you see, the only way you're ever going to get a father to stop haggling is if he is burnt enough times. To make this particular victory even sweeter, the £180 sword stick was confiscated at Istanbul airport and, with any luck, returned to the trader, so he could fleece another arrogant English haggler with an oversized ego and a loose grasp of both exchange rates and what items are allowed in your hand luggage.

Holiday Clothing

Clothes shopping on holiday can also be a big mistake. I hold my hand up and admit I've made some regrettable purchases in this department, whether it's the fake FC Málaga away shirt or a pair of those tie-dye baggy gap-year pants that make you look like an incontinent Cossack dancer. Any additions to your wardrobe made abroad will soon be regretted. If David Beckham, the world's most stylish man, couldn't pull off the sarong, what chance have you got? Still, I'll forgive you for wasting twenty quid on an 'I Love New York' T-shirt. What is unforgivable is any forays into cultural dress. Across the board it is unacceptable. From the humble clog to lederhosen, all the way up to the sombrero, there is never an excuse to start dipping your toe – or toes or more importantly head – into a national dress. At worst, you'll look like a racist. At best simply a twat.

This is an area where, once again, I'm afraid to say, my father has seriously let himself down on several occasions. On a family holiday in the Middle East he was on strict instructions to be respectful of their culture at all times. Travelling with my father to a Muslim country, in which they adhere to Sharia law, is a tense affair. Like taking a child with ADHD around a munitions factory, you're always on your guard. Forget worrying about what was in his hand luggage, we were worrying about him coming back with hands.

I had spent the holiday watching my father like a hawk, yet one lapse in concentration and he was lost into the souk. Michael Whitehall wandering around unattended is a terrifying prospect – forget bull in a china shop, it's more like a Rottweiler in a primary school – but not even I could have envisaged how disastrous it would prove to be. After about an hour of searching, I turned the corner to find him purchasing a dish-dash.

'Noooo!'

I hurried him away before he could start trying it on.

'I thought I could get your mother one of those burkas as well; that way she wouldn't get sunburnt like she always does.' I had thought Daddy would be against the burka, but a clash between feminism and Islam gives him real problems about who to support, like how I feel when Spurs play Chelsea.

And he doesn't learn.

'I'm blending in with the locals,' he said, as he strode around the bazaar in Istanbul, an overpriced sword stick in one hand and now a traditional fez on his head, looking like Tommy Cooper on a psychotic rampage.

Ten Things You Will Regret Buying on Holiday

1. The coconut leaf hat. Looks great on the beach, but not an item that travels well. You're basically wearing compost. Sat on the plane with it wilting round your head and something hatching in one of the mouldy leaves, you realise your 'wacky beach hat' is the carrier of Coronavirus 2.0.

2. Comedy T-shirts. I went to Vegas and all I got was this lousy T-shirt. Incorrect; you also got looks from everyone at the airport and the plane thinking that you are a knob. And given it's Vegas, possibly the clap.

3. Anything with the Pope on it. Italians love a bit of Pope tat. They will literally put his face on everything. Except condoms, obviously.

4. Electrical items. The fatal error of purchasing discounted electronic equipment abroad only to take it home and find out it's not compatible with anything you own, that switching on your new lamp carries about the same fire risk as spraying your home with kerosene and your new DVD player is about as much use as tits on a bull.

5. The Luk Thep doll. Native to Thailand, this creepy lifelike doll, which in the old days used to contain a human foetus (making it a revolting body-horror version of a Kinder Surprise), is without doubt the weirdest holiday souvenir you can buy, or in our case be given, anywhere in the world. It will not just traumatise you, it will also be a constant presence in your life, as indeed Winston has

been. If you want confirmation of this, look no further than the Instagram account my mother set up for him. A platform on which she persists in trolling me by dressing the doll up in my old baby clothes. I'd actually feel sorry for the little fella if it weren't for the fact he is an inanimate object made of plastic and human hair.

6. Anything phallic. I have fallen into the trap of buying novelty phallus-shaped keyrings, corkscrews, chocolates, even a scented candle. Then one holiday I was made to remove a penis-shaped bottle opener from my hand luggage; the bottle opener element had snapped off in my bag and I couldn't find it so it looked to everyone at customs like I was travelling with a massive wooden dildo in my hand luggage. So don't buy anything cock-shaped on holiday. Except condoms, obviously.

7. Wine. If you're in France, sure, maybe buy wine. But don't fall into the trap of travelling somewhere obscure, drinking a bottle of the local stuff and thinking you've unearthed the next great trend. Once your sanity returns and you're not giddy on holiday spirit and charmed by the nice local waiter, you will remember that there is a reason that Croatia is not one of the world-famous winemaking nations. Your friends will not necessarily thank you for turning up to their party with a case of Dubrovnik Pinot Noir.

8. Hawaiian shirt. Just about acceptable on the holiday itself (if said holiday is in Hawaii – they don't go down so well in Tehran), but they should be burnt before you travel home. Maybe that's why they make them out of such highly flammable material: they're giving us a hint.

9. Politically loaded memorabilia. This shouldn't need saying but we all know what certain fathers are like by now. If it's got Mussolini's face on it, put your credit card away. So as not to be done on a technicality, nothing with Chairman Mao, Kim Jong, Donald Trump or any other evil dictators for that matter. The worst example of this was buying some old Iraqi banknotes with Saddam Hussein on them. Whip one of those out by accident at the garden centre and you could get some very funny looks (mind you, it's even worse if the bloke on the till sees it and gives you a smile of approval). In fact, his penchant for slightly dodgy memorabilia is so prevalent that during lockdown any Zoom interview my father conducted always started with me calling my mum to make sure any backdrop he was seen in front of didn't have any of his souvenirs lurking on a shelf ready to get him cancelled.

10. Food. Just remember it always tastes better in the place you're in. There's no point lugging back a lot of Droëwors and biltong from South Africa, for example. If you have any old shoes back home, just rip the soles off them and chew on that instead; for a more authentic flavour, do it after you've taken a walk through a cowshed. Also, they have everything back home anyway. You've spent a three-hour flight back from Spain smuggling a length of chorizo in your pocket and had the woman sitting next to you complain to the air hostess that the man next to her is tenting an erection (to which I can only say I wish I was so blessed), only to walk into Waitrose that week and see the exact same brand of chorizo on offer.

Lost in Translation

A DESIGNATED FOREIGN-LANGUAGE speaker on the family holiday is essential, much like a designated driver. And much for the same reasons – everyone else will probably be too pissed to do it. Preferably, kids should club together and just hire a translator. Anything to avoid having to listen to your parents attempt to converse with foreigners in their own tongue on their own soil.

I used to struggle with languages when I first went to school. I was bottom of my French class – or, as the French say, 'le bottom'. Pretty sure that's right. It wasn't until I got into my more self-aware teenage years and started going on holidays abroad that I became conscious of how excruciating it was to observe my father addressing a Frenchman in French. Talking very loudly and slowly in broken English, as though the man was underwater; gesticulating wildly with his hands, as if he were not so much asking for directions

to the Carrefour as engaging in a game of charades. The hammer blow would land when the person he was talking to would respond in perfect English. There could be no greater incentive to learn a language. Maybe that's why they do it? I ended up with an A (as the French call it, 'un A' – amazing how it never leaves you) at GCSE French and I put this down to having had to sit through these shocking exchanges, wishing the ground would swallow me up or that the gods would strike my father dumb. Either way, I felt someone responsible needed to stop the madness and learn how to ask for directions to the swimming pool in La Rochelle.

'Daddy, you should at least try to make an effort with the language; we are in France,' I would say to him naively. Surely nothing could be worse than what I'd just seen. At least making an effort shows a little respect for their culture. Of course, what I failed to realise was that showing a little respect for French culture was the furthest thing from his mind. You might as well ask him to show a little respect for International Women's Day or non-binary pronouns.

'Garçon,' he would holler at the grown man waiting on us – the one looking as though he was picturing my father being politely shown not to his table but to the guillotine.

'Bring – me – my – bill. Merci.'

Faced with such a spectacle, you immediately realise why our two nations have fought quite so many wars.

Worse still is my father's propensity to slip into the accent. This is something he has always done – genuinely, I think – without realising it. I can't believe it's a conscious attempt to provoke World War Three. It's like he develops a sudden bout of Foreign Accent Syndrome every time he tries to order a takeaway. As children, the horror that would engulf

us when we realised he was about to order a Chinese, all three of us bolting towards the kitchen and diving through the air to grab the telephone receiver before he could unleash his misguided impression of Mickey Rooney in *Breakfast at Tiffany's* to whichever poor unsuspecting waiter at the Blue Dragon in Putney had answered the phone that night, and before the entire household got hauled up before the Equality and Human Rights Commission. We have warned him. I literally told him he's verging on yellowface; unfortunately, I think he thought I was talking about his liver.

This fear of accent slippage is amplified tenfold when you are in the country itself and you know that just one outing of the 'cod Asian' accent could see us getting chased down the street by an angry mob, or banged up abroad. Still a great chance to perfect that accent as you practise phrases like 'Can I speak to the British embassy?' and 'Can I please have another bucket, this one's full?'

While my dad's 'slippages', for the most part, seem accidental, my mother's attempts to talk as the locals are calculated and can be just as cringe. Especially when we were in the West Indies.

'You're a fifty-year-old white woman. If I ever hear you utter the words "wha gwan' again, I will disown you as my mother.'

We did have one holiday where my father had been shouting at us so much on the journey out that for the first two days of the trip he had lost his voice completely, thus rendering him completely unable to patronise anyone. It was definitely a price worth paying. Mummy said the enforced silence meant it was the first proper holiday she'd had in years. If there's any way you can bring about these

circumstances deliberately, maybe by goading a parent into a shouting match by asking for a pocket money uplift or by constantly running away from them at the airport, you will greatly increase your chances of avoiding any major diplomatic incidents.

Traditionally, at one end of the spectrum, you have the parent that makes no attempt to use the language. At the other end, you have the parent that thinks they are fluent. On the one hand, the defeatist; on the other, the deluded. No one has a higher opinion of my mother's language skills than my mother herself. Her faith in her own abilities is like a religious belief in that it's maintained despite the lack of any evidence to back it up whatsoever. She may once have had some razor-sharp skills. Unfortunately, it has been some time since these skills had a polish and at best I would describe them as a little rusty. Yet despite this, she still insists while abroad on diving into conversation with all the confidence of Tom Daley leaping from the top board, only to realise someone's emptied out the water seconds before a faceplant into the concrete.

It comes from a good place, as she's desperate to fit in and would sooner not get what she asked for than have to ask for it in English. It's possible that this is the reason she ate nothing but borscht for that week in Ukraine, because it was the only word she knew. In fact, I'm convinced half the things she buys in shops or orders in restaurants are not what she thought she was getting, but her cultural sensitivities are such that she refuses to back down or attempt to unpick the situation.

'Mother, did you know you were getting chicken terrine for dessert?'

'Yes. That's what I ordered. Just wanted some lovely raw meat to round off the meal. Yum, yum, yum. Now you two can have coffee while I tuck into a digestif prawn cocktail.'

One of my mother's more dramatic incorrect French phrases has gone down in family folklore. It was uttered by her in Provence on the occasion she accidently ran over my then baby brother with the hire car. She hadn't noticed that Barnaby had decided her backing the car out of the ridiculously small garage was an opportune moment for him to have a wander around the rear of the vehicle. A thud, a squeal, an emergency dash to the nearest hospital, and we were treated to a wonderful display of my mother's loose yet confident grip of the French language.

'Mon bébé est mort,' she screamed as she burst through the casualty-department doors with a now-giggling Barney cradled in her arms. He clearly wasn't 'mort' and luckily was pretty undamaged. As, indeed, to her relief, was the Espace, thereby avoiding the need for any further uncomfortable explanations in her woefully inadequate French when returning the car to the hire car company.

'Yes, I'm sorry about that dent; I tried to park it on my toddler's head. Does that mean mon deposit est mort too?'

What makes my mother's desperation to speak the local tongue at all times even more baffling is that the minute she hears an English voice, she hones in on it like a SWAT team. It's her secret superpower, as she can detect one from a mile away. This is a strange desire the English have when holidaying abroad: to befriend any other English party they come into contact with. Perhaps it's simply because they don't have the requisite language skills to befriend the locals. Or perhaps we're just looking for reinforcements if things get ugly.

No matter how objectionable the fellow Brits abroad may be, the mere fact that they are British is common ground enough for my mother to think she has forged a lifelong friendship. She could be sunbathing next to Fred and Rose West and she'd end up swapping email addresses with them and inviting them over for dinner or, worse still, my next gig. The amount of post-show green rooms I have been in where two people I have never clapped eyes on in my life sidle up to me and introduce themselves.

'Hello, we're the Wilsons.'

'Yes, of course you are. Sorry, remind me how I know you?'

'We met your mother in an internet café in Mallorca in 1998. She was trying to make the man behind the desk understand her while your father mimed the concept of dial-up networking.'

This is one of the few situations where my father's complete lack of interest in acquiring any new members to his ever-decreasing circle of friends – whittled down every year by death and the long-term effects of his character – comes in handy. He can spot my mother trying to befriend a couple of crashing bores at a hotel bar and torpedo it with devastating efficiency.

'Michael, this is Sue and Roger, they're from Croydon. Roger works for the Inland Revenue.'

'Pleased to meet you. Hilary, quick word, Barnaby has just emptied all of our luggage into the hotel pool.'

'Barnaby's our youngest, he's only twelve,' my mother chirps, desperately trying to reel her new friends back in.

'We should never have let him drink that sangria. Another night in the cupboard for him, methinks,' says Michael, as Roger and Sue scuttle off, never to be seen again.

When it comes to the language, though, the problem is, of course, parents are just too reluctant to embrace new technology, by which I mean anything that post-dates the reunification of Germany. There are apps now that can help with these things. Google has the ability to translate your order into any language in the world. In fact, Google probably knows what you want to order in the first place, maybe even before you know yourself, and that it's almost certainly not borscht. It probably even knows what ingredients there are in 'Egg'. Yes, it's nice to learn a few choice phrases and deploy them at the right moment – at least give a nod to assimilation – but the important thing is to learn that as soon as it starts to go tits up, you must fall back into the caring arms of technology. Make those algorithms work to your advantage.

One such incident that happened to me on holiday and still haunts me to this day is a classic example of how the language barrier can take you out like a trip-wire if you're ill prepared.

We were in Spain and had been recommended a restaurant that specialised in using ingredients from artisanal suppliers in the surrounding area. I can't remember where we picked up news of this place, but a cheesemonger would almost certainly have been involved. It had taken me and my mother days to persuade my father that it would be good to support the local economy – never a likely winner, since he sees other countries as competitors we would ideally be grinding into the dirt. He finally succumbed when I said that it would be my treat and that I would foot the bill. All was going well and we were happily chowing our way through a delicious array of the chef's exquisite and flavourful delicacies when I

needed to pop to the lavatory to use their facilities. I excused myself from the table and off I went.

Now, I don't want to be accused of oversharing and go into too much lurid detail (actually, the word 'lurid' is oddly appropriate on this occasion), but let's just say I had to *drop the kids off at the pool*. I did my business, got up, flushed the toilet and nothing happened. I yanked the chain again. Still nothing, three, four, five times. I tried to get it moving but the flush was broken. Oh dear; Houston, we have a problem. I considered leaving the many swimming siblings there and doing a runner, but it was such a lovely restaurant and it just didn't seem right. I'm a well-brought-up boy. The idea of doing a shit-and-run just didn't sit well with me. Also, of course, I remembered that I was in the chair for this one and knew that my father would take a very dim view of me 'taking a French leave' (to employ one of the many phrases he uses to spread global harmony on our travels), thereby meaning he would have to do the honours at bill-paying time. So, there was nothing for it, I had to bite the bullet and do the decent thing and inform a member of staff that there was a problem with their facilities. I went out and sheepishly got the attention of the charming Spanish waiter who had been looking after us all evening, and would have had no idea what he was letting himself in for. It was a busy service and he was tending to another table at the time and again, for a fleeting moment, I considered letting it go, but as I looked round the restaurant at its happy diners, including my family, I knew I couldn't subject one of those innocent holidaymakers to the monstrosity I'd left. So I plucked up my courage and took control of the situation.

Here is where the language barrier became a problem. I have no Spanish whatsoever (certainly not the kind of

specialised technical vocab this situation called for), the waiter had spoken barely a word of English all evening, so I knew this was going to be tricky. I ended up having to gesture to him, miming that he needed to come with me immediately. He apologised to the table he was in the middle of serving and followed me, all without us having exchanged a single word. I beckoned him into the cubicle, pointed into the bowl of the lavatory, went to flush . . . and the toilet burst into life straightaway and down the contents went. My heart skipped a beat. The waiter stood there, looking at me confused. What trickery were the gods playing on me? Why had it suddenly kicked into action? The poor waiter stared at me, trying to comprehend what was going on. Had this stranger really just invited him into the toilet to say goodbye to his turds? Did he think I was in some way trying to pay a compliment to the quality of his food? Food so good it required a proper send-off? Get the chef in as well; let's give that meal the farewell it deserves. I didn't even have the language to explain the situation, so then had to usher him back out, go back to the table and make sure I didn't catch his eye again for the rest of the night. My family were stunned by the size of the tip I left at the end. And on my return to London, I instantly invested in some Rosetta Stone language tapes.

Michael: USEFUL PHRASES TO LEARN IN ANY LANGUAGE

No, those aren't our children.

How much will it cost to make this problem go away?

We are all having the *prix fixe*.

Please can you give me the interweb code?

I want an upgrade immediately.

I'm afraid I don't understand a word you're saying. Perhaps you could write it down, preferably in English.

Where is your superior?

He is not a doll; his name is Winston!

No, officer, I will not lower my voice!

I'll pay half that price and we can shake on it.

Listen, darling, this is the most powerful passport in the world; I am not standing in that queue!

I'm sure all this stuff is lovely, but could you ask the chef if he could rustle up a couple of lamb chops, preferably Welsh.

I would like a large glass of white wine with my lunch, in a proper glass. Well, maybe a small one as we're in Romania.

You appear to have directed me to a lavatory used by farmyard animals. Could you kindly show me one reserved for humans?

I am not her father; this woman is my wife!

No, you may not purchase my wife for thirty camels. Fifty and I might start listening. Provided you take the children with you as well.

Where to Rest Your Weary Head

THE GREATEST MISCONCEPTION with a holiday is that by changing the family's environment you will suddenly see their behaviour transform as well. Suddenly because you're in a different country you're going to turn into the Waltons. Whereas in fact you're more like West Ham – home or away, you're still pretty much the same bunch of bastards. What you are actually doing is simply moving all your chaos from one set of four walls to another. That said, the nature of those four walls can have a significant effect on how much that chaos will be amplified, and also how much it will cost you if any of those walls get damaged.

Hotels

Standard practice is to book a hotel. On the surface this is the most convenient option: your every need catered for, beds

made daily, laundry services on tap, food available round the clock and a helpful concierge to act as a lieutenant to whichever parent is in charge.

But don't be fooled. To use a hotel metaphor, if you lift the sheets, you'll see the stains on the mattress beneath.

The first problem with the four walls of a hotel is the walls themselves. Because they always want to cram as many rooms into the building as possible, hotels always seem to make the dividing walls between rooms as thin as tissue paper. Which, in a communal living complex, is ill-advised. Many's the night I have spent tossing and turning, trying to entomb my head in a pillow in a futile attempt to block out the sounds emanating from the room next door. On one particularly traumatising overnight stay, not only could I hear my neighbours' intermittent guttural grunts and the sweaty slap of skin on skin – it honestly sounded like they were high-fiving on every thrust – but the walls were so flimsy, you could practically make out the occupants' breathing patterns and even the sound of someone's eyes rolling to the back of their head. I didn't sleep a wink. The following morning I vowed that I would never take the room next to my parents ever again.

As a result of this event, my advice to all families everywhere is: when booking a hotel, split up. Pick a big hotel, as it will have literally hundreds of rooms to choose from. Why would you want ones next to each other?

'I do like to know you're close at hand, Daddy – if I'm going to be woken up by someone taking a leak at three in the morning, I'd hate it to be a stranger.' At the very least, insist on separate floors, wings even. Better still, try to see if they have a sister hotel nearby. If you're in America, consider an adjacent state.

Parents are reluctant to do this, of course, as for them a hotel stay is never about relaxing, but yet another chance for gladiatorial combat in defence of their own bank balance. As well as taking it in turns to man-mark their children at all times to prevent any minibar-based catastrophes, it is also about clawing back as much value for money as they can over the course of the stay.

This will kick off on day one with breakfast. The family will be ferried down at 6.30 a.m., when they for some inexplicable reason start their breakfast service. Why is it hotels seem to be on a concerted mission to ensure none of their guests can ever get a lie-in? The only people who should ever have to see my father that early in the morning are my mother and, in extreme circumstances, a paramedic. If it isn't the early breakfast, it's the maid who lets herself into your room at ten o'clock, waking you up with a yelp, as blearily you open your eyes to discover you've kicked off the bedsheets in the night and are now sleeping with one leg over the duvet, butt up, presenting your bare bottom to a complete stranger, as if you think a prostate check is part of the turn-down service. It's made far worse by the fact that you haven't yet got your contact lenses in and you're as blind as a bat and unable to make out the identity of the woman you've just inadvertently put into therapy for the rest of her life, tormented by flashbacks every time she sees an overripe peach. This initial encounter means that for the remainder of your stay, you are unable to look, talk or even be in the same room as any of the maids, lest it be the one who has the image of your sprawled buttocks burnt onto her retinas for evermore.

Returning to the subject of the hotel breakfast, this is a meal it is impossible to miss: as it's the only meal included with the room rate, it's imperative for your parents to march you down

to the dining room like prisoners of war being dragged from their bunks. Whether you are hungry or not, you are forced to load up from the buffet – normally a collection of pastries, kiwi fruit, eggs done every which way (except foamed!) and wrinkly sausages that wouldn't even make the cut for an andouillette. These wrinkly dried-up buffet sausages will also give you an uncomfortable reminder of the noises that kept you awake last night from the room next door, as does, to be fair, the phrase 'done every which way'. The purpose of loading up from the buffet is to ensure that all subsequent meals taken outside the hotel will not make so much as a ripple in the holiday budget, as everyone is still hunched double with indigestion and stomach cramps, having had Mother pump gratis Bircher muesli down their throats like a foie gras goose.

In order to mitigate any hunger pangs that might rear their ugly heads, my mother also treats breakfast as a harvesting exercise for the rest of the day. She is at her most egregious when faced with a breakfast buffet. Bread rolls stuffed with the continental options, two solid weeks of ham and cheese. She sees the rule as being not 'All You Can Eat' but 'All You Can Possibly Conceal'. Because who needs to purchase a mid-morning snack when Mummy can hitch up her skirt and produce an unexpected brioche bun? She has been known to travel with her own paper napkins in tow, as even she draws the line at snitching the linen ones to conceal her breakfast booty back up to the bedroom. She has a shred of dignity, although not enough to prevent her from smuggling individually wrapped butter pats out of the restaurant under her sunhat. And why do you think the despicable, kleptomaniacal fiend carries so many fanny packs around?

The exhausting frugality spreads to the actual room as

well. The minibar is guarded like Fort Knox. If products are not on those sneaky-ass fridge sensors, then they will be removed by a parent and hidden in the safe. Tins of caramelised peanuts are treated with the reverence normally reserved for the Koh-i-Noor diamond. Without these measures we would run the risk of someone getting the munchies late at night and raiding the minibar, only for it to come back and bite them on check-out. I remember the one time it did happen, my father being handed an itemised bill on departure and being forced to pay £20 for a miniature tube of Pringles.

'This is coming out of your allowance; I told you to stop eating them.'

'Sorry, Daddy, it's not my fault – once you pop, you can't stop! Don't blame me, blame science.'

This doesn't mean to say the emptied minibar is redundant. Many parents love to cram it full of discounted items they've bought in the local supermarket. The whole thing becomes like a backlit jeweller's display cabinet full of cut-price meat and dairy, normally the exact same items they can get back home. So my advice is the minute you are through the door, repurpose your suitcase strap and luggage padlock and immediately wrap it around the minibar fridge and lock it shut for the duration of your stay.

As I alluded to earlier, the sad thing is though I'm loath to admit it, my attitude towards hotels has definitely been influenced by my mother. You can take the boy out of Putney, but – well, he'll probably come back to Putney sooner or later, carrying pretty much everything he's been able to lay his hands on like some sort of public-school-educated pack rat. My mother's ability to strip down a hotel room and steal as many of the contents as possible was learnt from the Sensei of such things,

her mother, and handed down, generation to generation, and it's definitely something that I have inherited. I find myself standing there wondering if the architrave is firmly glued on. I even try to rationalise it in my own head – 'I don't need these items; I'm lucky enough to be in a position where I could easily afford these things' – but the genetic kleptomania takes hold and I stride into the bathroom thinking, 'If these bastards are going to charge that much for Pringles and make me pay for Wi-Fi, those shower curtain rings are coming with me.'

And it's not just the obvious items I will go for. I think outside the box; obviously I take the toiletries, that tiny bottle of shampoo – you never know when you're going to need to wash one armpit. But thanks to my mother's influence, I'll take anything. Shower mats, light bulbs, linen, batteries from the television remote. I've found myself admiring the fire safety notice and thinking, 'That'd look lovely in our lounge.' I can't help it; it's in my DNA.

The other key bit of advice when stealing from a hotel that I have mastered over the years is not to fall into the trap of waiting until the end of the holiday to clear everything. Thievery is like any other job of work: you want to get it out of the way, then you can relax and enjoy yourself. You don't want to have to do it in a muck sweat as you depart. If you want to pilfer high-prize items, the key is to hit the ground running and blame the people that were in the room before you. The minute you check in, you call down to the front desk in a rage.

'Excuse me, madam, why an earth have I been put in a room with no television?' That's right, because it's already in my bag.

Mummy says it was much harder before they brought in flatscreens.

Michael's LETTER OF COMPLAINT

Now not all holidays of course go according to plan. Sometimes things do go wrong, and it's very important to give feedback. Here is an example of some feedback which I once gave to an establishment that we stayed in, where things weren't quite right.

Dear Major Sharples,

Being an ex-military man, I thought you might appreciate a debrief following our premature departure last Monday from your 'luxury family hotel'. Oxymoron comes to mind. You may also consider adjusting your terms of business to prevent scores of future guests charging for the lifeboats before the ship has sailed. My points as follows:—

1 Your family rooms are more akin to what I imagine prison accommodation was like in the 1960s I know that natural fibres were all but forgotten then but surely we have moved away from nylon and polyester, especially with regard to bedding. The set of iron beds were so tightly jammed together that the only way to reach the small window and close the synthetic curtains was to clamber over them. Ditto getting into the furthest away bed. The static created by this manoeuvre could have powered the lights; well had the bedside lamp not been missing it's bulb. And where were we expected to put our suitcases? We had to leave the door of our room open and put them in the corridor under the fire alarm which I noticed was switched off.

2. The family in the room next to us were clearly having as grim a time as we were. Not that we actually met them but owing to the wafer thin walls, we could hear their every conversation, including some very coarse expletives which I would certainly not use in front of my own children.

3. Given the cell like quality of the rooms, I was surprised that you hadn't installed searchlights in the grounds to prevent residents attempting to escape during the night. And the printed set of rules left in our room was beyond belief. The swimming pool, a more modest construction than the cleverly shot photograph in your brochure, despite the fine weather was only available to children between 9am and 10 am and 4pm and 5pm. Was this some kind of sick joke?

4. The claim in the aforementioned brochure that you were 'beachside' was more than a joke and more of a violation of the Trade Descriptions Act. Of which I'm sure you're aware. You are indeed 'beachside' if you are first prepared to walk across a large municipal car park, cross a busy road, head through a wooded area and then abseil down sheer cliffs with three children, two pushchairs and several wholly inadequate beach towels.

5. Your 1960s theme is sadly not restricted to the decor. I thought rissoles had made a very welcome disappearance shortly after wartime rationing ended. And tinned peaches and condensed milk as a suitable dessert for adults staying at a 'luxury' hotel? And you dared to put the words Haute Cuisine at the top of your menus. Do you know what those words mean? I'll tell you as you clearly don't. They mean 'The Cuisine of 'High level' restaurants serving gourmet food'!

6. I greatly disliked being presented with the same napkin during our stay, apparently a hotel tradition. I cannot understand why you would think it acceptable, let alone hygienic, to put a used napkin, in an envelope with my name on it. I would suggest that you invest in some more linen napkins or god forbid, switch to paper ones.

7. I'm sure staffing in the hospitality industry is testing but I think you should instigate some basic training particularly with staff whose first language is not English. My wife was addressed as 'lady' by a helpful but over familiar waitress on more than one occasion and the wine waiter used 'mate' as his usual form of address.

8. During your ridiculously early dinner service of 6pm to 7.30 p.m, your staff should not be laying up vacated tables for breakfast. This ruse is clearly designed to rush guests through the meal and get them back into their cells before lockdown. Well it didnt work with us; We will finish our dinner in our own time.

9. Having endured two nights at your hotel, I now fully understand why you insist on full payment in advance and I regret that it was necessary for so much shouting and unpleasantness before I was able to secure a full refund from you. Having cowered in your back office and only come out when I had to speak frankly to your charming receptionist, I'm glad that the matter was ultimately resolved.

I hope that you and your staff will benefit from these remarks and find them of use in the future.

Yours sincerely,

Michael Whitehall.

Villas

If hotels are too restrictive, then the other option is the self-catering villa. 'Villa' is an Italian word meaning 'money pit operated by a scam artist'. Most images for any holiday villa are a homage to the art of the photographer. They say the camera never lies – well, it can bullshit. The 'sea view' that is only visible when leaning out of an upstairs window, craning around to the left and if you happen to be travelling with the Hubble telescope. The pool, always photographed from a low angle, thereby giving it Olympic proportions when, in fact, it is only just longer than the paddling pool you have left on the lawn at home. It's so small it's impossible to push off into a breaststroke without busting your nose on the opposite side. The verdant garden, with the beautiful, lush, evergreen hedge running along the side of the property. What the photographer has cleverly cropped out is the eight-storey block of flats on the other side, with literally hundreds of windows overlooking your villa's al fresco dining area and swimming pool, so that it's impossible to so much as change into your trunks without being greeted by a round of applause. The view from the terrace, with what looks like rolling fields just over the boundary, fields that actually turn out to be an industrial landfill site. Villa photography is essentially a form of catfishing. And to extend that analogy a little further, more often than not the glamorous elegant model you think you're turning up to meet will turn out to be a decrepit snaggle-toothed sex pest who hasn't got a shower.

The descriptions are just as bad – literature that would make even an estate agent blush. The villa that's 'handy for

the airport' – by 'handy' they mean literally at the end of the runway. It only took you two minutes to get there from the plane but you will now be woken up every morning by a minor earthquake when a Boeing 747 tears past your window. And much like the hire car mania, most of the time in a villa will be spent not enjoying the facilities but living in fear of losing that hefty deposit. You either accept you're going to forfeit that sum of money after two weeks staying there with a messy family of five or accept that you're probably going to have to spend the exact same amount as you put down in the first place getting in the team of industrial cleaners they used to scrub down the Ecuadorian embassy after they booted out Julian Assange.

Camping

The more daring families might opt to forgo bricks and mortar altogether and brave . . . a campsite. Like a hotel but with no breakfast, rooms or anything to steal other than the goat in the next field who won't fit in your suitcase without serious protest.

The only camping expedition we went on as a family ended up with a slightly bizarre arrangement. My father had reluctantly agreed to join his wife and children on a trip to Cornwall. A fair amount of negging him had taken place in the weeks preceding, filling his head with images of us all sluicing ourselves in a stream and spit-roasting a squirrel over a camping stove. He was desperate to prove his mettle, especially as I think I'd also put it into his head that my friends' younger dads would not be fazed by such an excursion and that, maybe, it was his advancing years – this

was decades ago, when he'd only just got his free bus pass – that meant he was afraid of camping. Some bluster about him having been a Boy Scout, I think he knew Lord Baden-Powell personally, and a few calls to his secretary to clear his diary, and we were on the road.

My father was now ready to prove to us all that he had a touch of the Bear Grylls beneath that haughty façade. Unfortunately, his role of gentleman-adventurer was short-lived. One look at the campsite's bathroom facilities, which amounted to a shared tap and a ditch, and Daddy about-turned out of the field, saying he wanted to go to a hotel. Nice one. That's not entirely true. He did at least stay to help us put up the tent. I say 'help'. He sat in the car with the heating on and barked out orders from the instruction manual, as my mother and I did the back-breaking work of actually assembling it. The boots on the ground to his Eagle's Nest. As he explained to us, some people are born to lead, and those same people are absolutely not born to douche them-selves with a hose. He then had my mother drop him at a nearby bed and breakfast, where he remained for the rest of the holiday, only occasionally stepping out from his cosy room to visit us when the Test match broke for tea.

I am not dismissing this arrangement. It actually worked out rather well: we could see him for mealtimes and the odd bath, and then return to the campsite without him when we wanted to have any actual fun. I'd highly recommend it if you're heading off camping and want to ensure your dad gets his space, for his peace of mind and, frankly, yours.

In Sickness and in Poor Health

FROM THE TIME I fused my finger to a car cigarette lighter on the way to the airport to the unfortunate fall I suffered when climbing into our Mitsubishi Shogun in a pair of my sister's high-heeled Disney princess shoes, breaking my fall with my face and getting a pair of shiners to start the holiday off with, many of our family holidays have ended up resembling the opening scenes to an episode of *Casualty*. Now, I am not a doctor. It's a thorn in my parents' side, and the reason they get upset at family weddings, as well as being reminded that my medically unqualified testicles have still not sired them a grandchild. All my uncles, aunts and cousins are doctors. It's the noblest of professions. At least my grandmother thought so and loved reminding everyone. I was off telling dick jokes in pubs while my cousin Tom was saving lives. Although, as I wanted to point out, he's a GP in the sleepy Hampshire village of Upper Buttfucknowhere. I suspect on a

day-to-day basis there is more bunion-removing than actual life-saving. Pointing that out would have fallen on deaf ears – another thing he has to tend to a fair bit, I imagine. Still, I think I have never felt further away from a profession than medicine. You might suggest prostitution, but I'd say you're not sufficiently familiar with my corporate work. This is a roundabout way of me saying any medical advice I dispense should probably be taken with a large dose of caution.

Your health when travelling is of paramount importance. But I also think it's worth remembering that medical science is subjective. The problem with parents is that there is always going to be a degree of fussing. My mantra is: unless something's literally about to fall off or explode, it can probably wait. And if it does fall off or explode, then to some extent the problem's cleared itself up. I know that is not sage medical advice. It's probably an approach that will catch up with me one day. I'll be up a mountain somewhere having my appendix removed with a spork.

While I totally get the 'safe not sorry' mantra, surely when on holiday it can be: 'Safe *once you get back to England* not sorry'. You always need to weigh the urgency of any medical intervention against the time it takes up, time that you could have spent on more essential activities like sitting by a pool drinking daiquiris. My mother is not of this opinion; in fact, she seems to be on a mission to see every A&E department in Europe, like they're notches on her wheelie metal-framed bedpost. She's always had the belt-and-braces approach to the human body and can be a bit of a doomsayer. She's got the optimism of a Radiohead album and the bedside manner of an undertaker. A light sniffle is definitely the early signs of some rare tropical bug that's been

Couple of gap year tragedies

Daddy always on my back . . .

Michael realises he can't swim.

Michael kicking back and tucking into a nice fun book about a Facist collaborator

Michael with his beloved child and mule

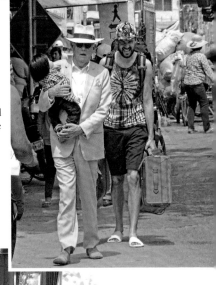

No matter how many travels, we're never tired of each other's company (series one, episode one)

Uber in Romania leaves a little to be desired.

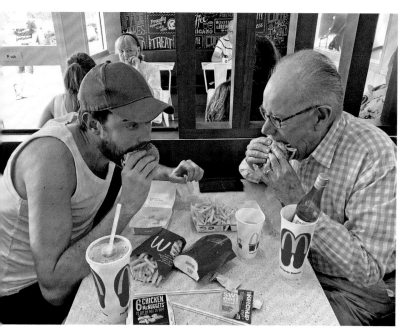

I'm lovin' it. He's hatin' it. At least he got to smuggle in a McChardonnay.

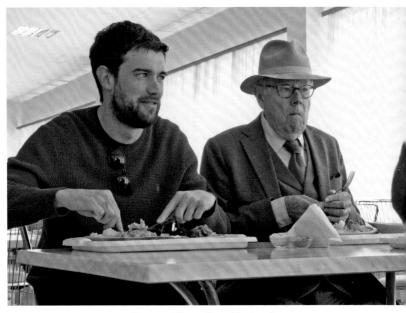

First rumblings of trouble ahead . . .

Waiting to settle our bill at Chernobyl Hospital, which was sadly not Bupa-accredited

What's the Turkish for 'saw you coming a mile off'…?

addy joining in the fun at naked yoga

What happens in Vegas stays in Vegas –
apart from Hilary's 1,000 selfies.

If you think this is basic, wait until you see the rail bus replacement service!

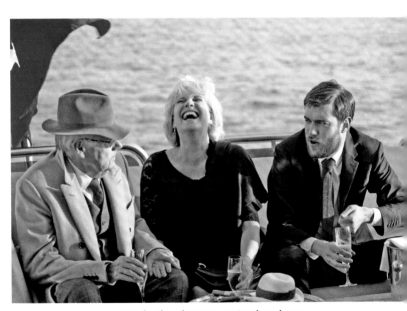

My mother has always appreciated our humour.

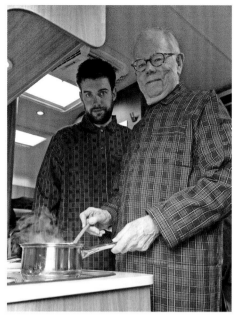

If the caravan's a-rockin', please do come a-knockin'
as Daddy could be having a medical emergency.

dog mother in her shrine

Even in Christmas games, Jeremy Corbyn
gets to live rent-free in Daddy's head.

Barney was sent to his room after this photo for not adhering to the dress code.

Nicking five identical bicycles was quite an achievement.

contracted from not following her instructions to avoid the tap water. In fact, anyone caught even approaching the sink with a glass in their hand is likely to get rugby-tackled to the floor. Sunstroke is talked about as if it were an actual stroke, which, if not properly treated, might take years of rehabilitation. Weil's disease, which mothers seem to be more worried about that any other condition in existence, is never far from their minds, ditto Lyme disease. Although there always seems to be a good few degrees of separation in their 'firsthand' anecdotal evidence – it's someone's cousin or a friend of a friend that got Weil's disease on holiday and dropped dead. I posit that no mother has ever actually met anyone who got Weil's disease, let alone died of it. I'm not even sure that it's such a big deal – I looked up the symptoms and they include nausea, listlessness and involuntary weeping, and I get all of those on a family holiday anyway. Still, my mum is always on the lookout for any potential host. 'Barnaby, do not lick that broom!' she barked at my brother (eighteen at the time). 'Our plumber's wife's neighbour's son got Weil's disease from eating dirt and now he's fed through a tube and pees in a bag. Do you want to pee in a bag, Barnaby?'

Woe betide any child that swallows a foreign object abroad. Into the rental car we go, off to find a highly trained professional to retrieve the small plastic toy soldier from their stomach like a human Kinder Surprise. My dad is far more of the 'wait to shit it out' school of thought. Not just with potential choking hazards but also when it comes to any bodily malfunctions abroad; for him it's all about holding your nerve. As a child, I could have come in from the pool carrying one of my severed fingers and he would have had my mother put the digit in the freezer and patch up

the wound with a plaster so we could get it sewn on by the NHS as and when we returned home. Actually, that's a little unfair: he would definitely have Hilary check the small print of the travel insurance coverage to see whether it was going to be a case of a costly trip to a foreign hospital or a tricky conversation with his son to assure him that three fingers on a hand is ample and the thumb is mainly for show. The only time I've ever seen my father genuinely distressed about an injury to one of his 'children' was when Winston, his good-luck doll, 'accidentally' got put in a suitcase by someone (me) that ended up going in the hold on a quite turbulent Ukraine Airlines flight. Unfortunately, when we got to the hotel in Kiev and my father unpacked, he discovered Winston's head and body in different corners of the suitcase. There would have been waterworks had his tear ducts not dried up and sealed over many moons ago. I had to call an admittedly slightly baffled concierge and have him bring some cable ties and Gorilla Glue to my father's suite so that he could perform some amateur surgery. I tried to tell him that maybe putting Winston out of his misery would be the most humane thing to do – a sack and some rocks and a long swim at the bottom of the Dnieper River – but Michael was having none of it. Frankenstein's baby lived to see another day.

I've had enough experiences of hospitals abroad to know it's best to try to stay out of trouble. In India on my gap year (I say 'year' but it actually lasted about eighteen months; it took me a long time to find myself – I may still be out there some-where) a friend crashed a motorbike and ripped open the side of his leg. It was technically a scooter, but he only gave me permission to tell this story if I embellish it to make it sound less pathetic. This vicious, near-fatal high-speed collision,

which happened on a dangerous highway at rush hour (thank goodness he hadn't simply taken a corner too quickly after replenishing our supplies of Supernoodles . . .), resulted in my one and only experience of a rural Indian hospital. Luckily I was unscathed. I'd been on the back of the scooter at the time of the collision, straddling him tightly as I was quite scared; he was in such a vice-like grip between my thighs that when we came off the scooter he landed beneath me and broke my fall. I feel like this may be the detail of the story he was most eager to omit. But I think it paints a powerful picture.

The doctor looking after my friend spoke very little English but he was a fan of the 'Indian head shake', a simple, universal gesture that I later came to understand meant 'yes' or 'good'. This is something I wish I'd known at the time, as it can be extremely unnerving to see a doctor shake his head from side to side when you've just asked him if your friend is going to be able to keep his leg. And why was he doing it so cheerily? I thought. Did I cry because I thought my friend's leg was going to be amputated? Yes, I did. Did I look quite stupid when he literally *strolled* out ten minutes later with no stitches and a small plaster on his shin? Very much so. I maintain I only teared up because I was worried about how we'd get the Supernoodles back to the hostel.

Noah – of course the guy I went on my gap year with is called Noah (admittedly, only because Montague had to back out at the last minute) – was absolutely fine. Anyway, I read this bit out to him last time we had lunch and asked him if it was OK – he shook his head so I'm assuming that means yes.

In Kauai, it was a dislocated rib. It's a loaded injury. I've read enough urban myths about pop stars to know that. How do you explain this away? A young man in his hotel

room, away from home, away from his girlfriend, bored, lonely, frustrated. What sordid experiments in onanism could possibly have resulted in such a displacement? I will admit, at the time I was jacked up on some pretty powerful painkillers; maybe that wasn't helping the paranoia. Yet, the truth was, if anything, staggeringly even more embarrassing than my most lurid fiction.

A trip to the hotel gym had once again ended with me bypassing the weights and anything else that looked too much like hard work in favour of an exercise bike tucked away in the corner. Now, usually I would pop on an audio book and lose myself in a Hilary Mantel to get into my groove, gently pootling away on that bike like one of the characters from *Call the Midwife*. Everyone else is roaring round the velodrome; I'm taking a turn about the village, pinging my bell at the vicar. But on this occasion, unfortunately, I'd forgotten to charge my phone. As luck would have it, the bike I'd chosen had a built-in TV set. I flicked through a few channels of American sports that I don't understand and then some American news stations which I understand even less, until I chanced upon a movie, *50 First Dates* – a glossy rom-com starring Adam Sandler and Drew Barrymore – just the ticket. To say I was engrossed in this film would be an understatement. An hour I spent hunched double over that exercise bike, desperately squinting at the subtitles, hanging on every word of this will-they-won't-they. Actually, technically, it's more of a will-they-won't-they-did she-remember-they. I was burning calories and emotions all at once, when suddenly I felt an excruciating pain in my ribcage, like I'd been stabbed. I literally collapsed off the bike onto the floor. There was a split-second when I considered

that, maybe, I'd suffered an actual broken heart, having just watched a terribly sad scene where Drew Barrymore's character Lucy experienced yet more rejection at the hands of the quite wicked Henry Roth. I reasoned with myself that perhaps it was a real medical condition. Still, as I lay there stricken like a turtle on its back in the hot sun, I knew I was in trouble. I didn't even have the possibility of Adam Sandler's love to revive me. When the cleaner walked in and found me crumpled, I was, thankfully, just close enough to the bench press that it conceivably looked as though I'd injured myself on one of the grown-up machines. Or had perhaps received a right hook from a personal trainer in a fit of roid rage.

Anyway, off to A and E, where a doctor asked me what I was doing at the time of the injury. Had I been in an awkward position for a long period of time? Don't blame me, I thought, blame George Wing (the screenwriter of *50 First Dates*) for his riveting rat-a-tat-tat dialogue. The drama was so captivating it had literally displaced one of my ribs. Dislocating a rib watching a Drew Barrymore movie on an exercise bike is a hard thing to recover from in every sense. And you can't start to get cagey when people ask you how you put out a rib alone in a hotel room. It's a story you need to get watertight or else, as I have already alluded to, people start filling in the gaps.

The reality is that most of the knocks and bangs we pick up on holiday tend to be a bit embarrassing, so always make sure you've got a good alibi when you return home bandaged together. Skiing a black run: that's my go-to. Admittedly, that was a harder sell with the 'Barrymore Incident' as I'd been in Hawaii at the time. Come to think

of it, I probably should stop referring to it as the Barrymore Incident if I don't want people to jump to sordid conclusions. Not helping either.

Unfortunately, some medical disasters come with receipts. I was in Cambodia when I developed a rather nasty rash on my buttocks. Not a life-or-death situation, but it was pretty unsightly. I decided that I needed some assistance, so I called the family GP back home. He told me I had two options: either I could find someone locally to give me the once-over or, if I'd prefer – and it's an interesting use of the word 'prefer' here – I could take a photograph of the offending area and send it to him via email so he could diagnose the problem from London. Hmm ... decisions, decisions. Well, given those two *horrific* options, I thought I'd probably rather send a picture of my arse to the family doctor (while realising I didn't have the skills of a villa photographer required to convey the most enchanting views of this particular property), rather than find some random guy in Cambodia and spread 'em. (I say 'random guy'; obviously, I would have found a medical professional, not strode into a wet market and dropped my kecks. 'Hey, chaps, anyone know what I should put on this?')

Next came the problem of actually taking the picture. You don't need me to tell you it was an incredibly awkward photo to have to take, and not in a 'how best to light this composition' kind of way. The thought of asking my father for assistance crossed my mind but was quickly discarded, frankly with something of a shudder. I decided that the best approach involved the bathroom mirror. I propped my bottom up on the sink and then tried to take a snap of my reflection, craning my head over my shoulder to see what I was doing.

I looked at the first attempt and it resembled something you might find on Kim Kardashian's Instagram feed. Though my bottom wasn't quite that swollen, throwing my head back over my own shoulder certainly gave the shot an unintended air of the seductive. There was far too much of a 'come hither' vibe to the whole thing. 'I can't send this to my doctor,' I thought. 'I'm trying to get a diagnosis, not slide into his DMs.'

My second attempt was less likely to break the internet, more likely to break my pelvis. I opted to put the camera into selfie mode, place it on the floor facing upwards and then squat over the lens as if I had just crapped out an iPhone. What then ensued must have looked like some hideous game of one-man naked Twister. I bobbed up and down, slut-dropping onto my phone as I tried to get low enough to press the button (and with my finger, not any other part of my anatomy). At one point, I realised that the camera was in video mode. That is not footage I would ever wish to see again. I live in terror of it unexpectedly surfacing, perhaps during an appearance on *Graham Norton*. Eventually, I managed to manipulate myself into a pose where I could take the picture. I looked at the image. It is singularly the worst, most unflattering picture of myself I have ever seen. The sooner this gruesome episode was over the better, I thought, so I fired off the email to my doctor and sat down to wait . . . Well, stood: it was quite sore to sit down at this point. Ten minutes passed with no response. 'It's fine,' I thought. 'He's probably cross-checking the image with some medical journals. It probably took him a good few minutes just to get over the initial shock.' Twenty minutes went by, and by now I'd started to get worried. An hour later and I was a

wreck, imagining the worst-case scenario in my head. I've got bum cancer, is that a thing? Can you even get it on your butt cheeks? I started imagining a line-up of comedians performing a benefit in my memory, perhaps with a big picture of me on the stage and the words 'Arse Relief'. Not how I'd ideally have chosen to be remembered. Oh my God! Maybe my mother was right and it's Weil's disease! All that naysaying and mockery, and now it has literally come back to bite me on the arse. Eventually, I gave in. I called him up and I said, 'Doc, put me out of my misery. What's wrong with me?'

And he said the worst thing you could possibly hear in that situation. He goes, 'Jack . . . I'm still waiting for the picture.'

My whole world went into soft focus; my heartbeat must have ground to a halt. All the worst-case scenarios flashed before my eyes. I knew that as so many celebrities have found out before me, once a picture of your arse is out there in the world, there's very little way to control it. Reeling, I hung up and went into the outbox of my emails. To my horror, I saw that I had indeed sent the email but, in my hurry to fire it off, I had not spotted that my phone had auto-filled in the email address from a Dr Stein to a Dr Stephens.

Phew, some of you are thinking, at least you sent it to another medical professional, a chance to get a second opinion, maybe? In the rarefied medical world of arse studies, the more expertise involved the better. That would be the case if Dr Stephens, the unwitting recipient of the pictures, were a doctor of medicine. Dr Stephens is, in fact, a doctor of art history! He is a professor at a university that I had applied to some ten years ago and was rejected from. I have had no contact with this gentleman for over a decade. How bizarre a morning must he have had? There, in his lecture hall, giving

a seminar on the Rococo period when, all of a sudden, *that* drops into his inbox! 'Ah, Jack Whitehall – shame things didn't work out for him here, but he's clearly done all right for himself. I wonder how he's been keeping?' He could only have logically assumed that, for the past ten years, I had been simmering, masterminding my revenge for the rejection, lurking in the shadows, waiting for the perfect moment to spring forth and troll him, completely out of the blue, on a Tuesday morning with a picture of my inflamed arsehole!

He never did respond. To this day, I have an email in my drafts somewhere, in which I was going to pass off the picture as a piece of abstract art that I was thinking of purchasing and wanted his opinion on. 'I've come across this piece, and I'm struggling with the attribution. Could it be a genuine Rothko?'

So, I think the advice I'd give you is: if in doubt – grin and bear it. But as I say, I'm not a doctor. Of any kind.

I realise that for older readers tales of gap-year tragedies and bum selfies may have lost you. Don't worry: Michael's on hand with some stories about ailments of his own that can win you back. Any gout lovers, you're in for a treat. Charge those glasses with port and put your best foot forward, it's time for an entire section dedicated to gout.

Michael: GOUT

I am constantly amazed by the body's capacity to hijack you at the most inopportune of moments; it has always been my worst enemy – with the exception of other theatrical agents – but I am also amazed by its capacity to fix itself,

either with the aid of medication or, more mysteriously, on its own. I try to remember, when I am laid low by some ailment, that as quickly as it may come on, it can also disappear with minimal intervention.

One example of this, which dogged me into my late thirties, was acid indigestion. I would never go anywhere without at least a couple of Rennies in my pocket, such was the inevitability of being struck down with heartburn, baffling many of those who had negotiated with me in show business, who might well have assumed I had no such organ at my disposal. Then I hit forty and, as if by magic, it disappeared. It just went. Weirdly, Jack finds himself on a similar trajectory with heartburn, but I am able to reassure him that he only has eight more years to go before it disappears! Acid indigestion and short sight, he likes to tell people, are two afflictions he inherited from me. He doesn't say anything about the wit and charisma, but I think those lie dormant in Jack, waiting to skip a generation. I think deep down he's just a bit upset that the generous proportioning in the trouser department was inherited by his brother and not him.

Another annoying ailment that had a habit of biting me on the foot, at the most inconvenient of moments, was gout. Jack, to my mind, seems to have a somewhat unhealthy interest in this condition, as you will have already noted from his constant references to it. I'm sure this is because gout is one of those ailments that everyone thinks is a joke. It has a silly name and joke connotations; it is largely deemed to be self-induced as a result of overindulgence and rich living, as if this is something I can help – they're just unavoidable hazards that have been thrust upon me as a result of my employment, the way I'm told the black lung is for

miners. Viewed this way, I think people would be a lot more sympathetic. Port tends to be one of the main guilty culprits, unfortunately also a drink with comic potential. It doesn't help that the two poster boys of this disease are Henry VIII and Luciano Pavarotti (though it hardly need be said, both very influential men and unexpectedly popular with the ladies). It really needs someone like Usain Bolt or Leonard Di Cappuccino to come out and say they've been getting a few flare-ups to give it some better PR. Other conditions with similarly comedic names are shingles (no fun at all), bunions (excruciating) and chilblains (ditto).

While no father would actively wish gout upon their son, I would love Jack to experience it for just a day. That way, he might have a little more compassion towards the gout-suffering community and know exactly what it feels like to walk in their extremely uncomfortable shoes. For a decade before I was able to get it under control with the help of regular medication (I have never had any time for the modern faddish theories about reducing one's alcohol consumption), it blighted several holidays. I could never understand why I wouldn't have an attack for months and then as soon as I found myself on holiday, boom, it would strike.

On one particular villa holiday in France, with two sets of family friends – one set being doctors and the other American, the husband of whom was on his second outing at parenthood and was even older than me (one should never discard the pencil while it can still be written with) – the gout was particularly trying. As a result, I was forced to wear a pair of what my children christened my 'grandma slippers' for the entire trip.

American Dad was not only older than me but he was

one of those exhaustingly enthusiastic travellers who like to organise every minute of every day and insist that everyone adhere to their schedule. Every morning at breakfast, the table would be covered with maps, guidebooks, clippings from the Travel Section of the *New York Times* and friends' handwritten recommendations for the area. He would then inform us of that day's proposed schedule. This was frustrating not only on account of there being a schedule in the first place, but also because, being an American, every time he mentioned said schedule, he pronounced it incorrectly. Having to endure this while clad in my grandma slippers I think symbolised how far the British as an empire has fallen.

My gout curtailed any kind of involvement in most of the appalling things he had planned: trips to the beach, a tour of a local brewery, visiting Roman ruins and, most especially, Hilary's badminton competitions. But it was mightily annoying having to sit as a passive spectator, nursing my elevated, throbbing foot, while watching my older American compadre leaping around the badminton court. I got no sympathy from anybody, not even the doctors we were on holiday with (in my experience, doctors don't tend to offer medical advice when on holiday), who merely joined in with all the mockery directed at me.

The apotheosis of this sorry state of affairs was when it was decided that we would do a Family Awards ceremony at the final dinner of the holiday (an awards ceremony that to the best of my memory was not much of a meritocracy and involved more than one or two stitch-ups). At last, having been sidelined all week, here was my moment to get involved. I am usually quite good at public speaking and at that time of our lives I was the comedian of the family,

as Jack was still at school and hadn't yet honed his comedy chops up to my level (in all honesty, we live in hope for things to change).

With a great flurry of excitement, my children introduced me as the evening's Master of Ceremonies. I would have been anxious not to disappoint them had I not been certain in my own mind that for me to do so was an impossibility. I don't know whether it was the three large glasses of Côtes du Rhône that I had consumed – for once I was taking good care to stay hydrated – or my exuberance to get going and finally make some sort of contribution to the holiday; whichever it was, as I stood up to begin my oration, my swollen foot attached itself to the wrought-iron leg of the table, catapulted me head first onto the paved terrace and briefly knocked me out.

So much for my big moment, cut down to size by my gout, my grandma slippers and hubris at my desire to get one over on my American friend, who had been upstaging me all week. It was lucky that our doctor friend was forced to do what doctors like least, and attend to a patient. Once I had come to he gave me a clean bill of health, and I was able, at long last, to get proceedings under way. Albeit it was not my most sparkling performance, owing to the minor concussion I had sustained. But even carrying a head injury, the result was still some way ahead of Jack presenting the BRITs.

I now take daily medication to keep the whole nasty business at bay, despite my rather severe GP suggesting the other day that, as I hadn't had an attack for nearly ten years, it might be time to come off the preventative drug. How very dare she! She is clearly not a gout sufferer herself, or she would never have come up with such a ludicrous suggestion.

'Madam,' I replied as authoritatively as I could, 'do you not think that it is precisely because I have been taking the pill that I haven't had an attack for ten years and that therefore, it is doing its job?'

She reluctantly concurred. I was so rattled by the exchange that I went home that evening and had to draw myself an extra-large glass of port to calm myself down.

Try New Things

WHEN TRAVELLING ABROAD, it's important to try new things. Broaden your horizons. I have always been willing to give anything a go, but it has taken a fair bit of trial and error to discover that there are some experiences best given a wide berth. Especially if you are travelling with your parents. It seems silly even to write this, and indeed, reading it back, I wonder what I was thinking in the first place, but top of the list of activities that are best avoided with your parents is: naked yoga.

'As an actor, you control where the audience is looking. The minute you take your kit off, you've lost them.' This was advice dispensed to me by Sir Michael Caine when I told him that I didn't think I'd done a job yet where I hadn't taken off my clothes. That said, I think I once read an interview with his *Dark Knight* co-star, Christian Bale, who said the great actors are willing to lay themselves bare. Now I come to think about it, maybe I took that quote a little too literally. I mean,

everyone agrees Dame Judi Dench is marvellous and you don't see her getting them out much these days, other than in *Cats* but it doesn't really count if you're covered in CGI fur. Still, there are porn actors who have shown less flesh on camera than me. Most of my contracts have a strict nudity clause in them: 'Jack will only appear in this show if he's allowed to get his kit off.' My arse has been on screen so much it has its own IMDb page. It gets recognised in gyms and changing rooms around the world. That's not strictly true, but when someone recognises me at a urinal, which is an awkward situation that happens with surprising regularity, the worrying thought always crosses my mind that this person didn't seem to know who I was until I dropped my trousers.

Apparently, I have always been this way inclined – 'not a shy boy', as my father puts it. My exhibitionism reared its ugly head at a very early age. My mother spent many a family holiday having to apologise to her friends for my streaking around the villa. One set of American friends had quite severe twin daughters, who took particular exception to my bursting into their room early one morning and performing a little rendition of my famous windmill dance. It's quite the big production number – Magic Mike could learn a lot. I was accused of being some kind of sinister pervert, and the twins never really looked at me the same way again. I should add that I was five years old when this incident occurred. I probably should have led with that fact – and at the age I'm at now, I guess it might be time to retire the windmill dance – but surely at age five, it's just harmless fun. My material has matured since then; I only resort to the windmill dance now if a gig's going really badly.

To be fair, my mother is not really fazed by the dangly bits.

I remember being in a hotel with her in Turkey. We went down to use the spa facilities, though failed to read a discreet sign that pointed out clothing was only an optional requirement. In a sense, I suppose clothing is always optional; it's just pretty obvious which of the two options you should be taking. I struggled to keep a straight face when an elderly Swedish couple joined us, sans costumes, in the sauna. I didn't think nudity could ever faze me until I came face to face with it next to my mum. I mean, literally next to her. At one point it nearly rested on her shoulder like a bald parrot. I think it dawned on both my mother and me at the same time that, clearly, we had missed the aforementioned small but vital piece of signage about the spa's dress code or lack thereof and that, perhaps, it was us, sitting in our swimming costumes, who were committing the violating sauna etiquette. It didn't go through my mind for a second, but a look flashed across my mother's face and I knew she was considering whether we should disrobe so as not to make our Scandi friends feel uncomfortable. I think the hard, cold stare I sent back in her direction put paid to this reprehensible notion.

My father tells me that, for as long as there is breath in his body, he will remember the terrifying noise the V-2 rockets made during the Blitz. The low hum as they whirred overhead before raining down terror and destruction upon the city below. A scary and long-lingering sound that will haunt him for ever. I think my V-2 rocket is the noise that Swedish man's testicles made as they hit the hot wooden bench of the sauna and began to gently fry like button mushrooms in a wok. The only thing worse than the sound of a man's balls hitting the steaming bench of a sauna is the sound they make when they come off it.

As Michael Caine would say, the Swedish man had very much lost control of his audience. I was unable to focus on anything else and, believe me, not for lack of trying. I tried to close my eyes and go to my happy place, but every time I went to my happy place I would find there was a Swedish man sitting there with his cock out. I tried to distract myself by fixing my gaze firmly on the thermometer in the corner of the room, willing it to spike to an acceptable level for me and my mum to get out of the smoggy genital-laden cabin. Perhaps it would get so hot that he'd have to leave or risk bollockburn (I think that's a medical condition, although it might be a place in Scotland). Then, just as I was about to make for the exit and a very cold shower – I don't know whether it's possible to rinse images out of your mind, but I was going to have a seriously good try – my mother decided to strike up a conversation with them! I mean, I know she loves a chat, but don't talk to the naked strangers, for crying out loud.

'Are you here for business or pleasure?'

What a ridiculous question. Obviously pleasure – look at them, woman! Also, is that really the sort of question you ask a couple of naked people? It sounds a bit like you're touting for some sort of trade.

The Swedish couple were only too willing to engage her in idle chit-chat; of course they did, nattering away about where they had been on their travels, which other cities they had been terrorising with their sweaty privates. I remained stoic, unwilling to engage, letting my mother cover every Swedish stereotype she could hastily assemble from her flat-pack of clichés. The Swedish man, who had a bushy blond moustache (I don't know why I needed to add that detail at

this juncture; for some reason it makes what he then said to me even creepier), leant towards me and gave a nod in my mother's direction and then purred, with a suggestively arched eyebrow, 'She's a lovely lady. You're a very lucky guy.'

My internal monologue went into overdrive. 'Oh my God! He thinks we're a couple! They're probably swingers. It figures. What kind of clientele do you expect to meet in a naked sauna? And, sorry, more importantly back to the fact that he thinks Mummy and I are an item, gross! I mean, what vibes are we giving off?'

With this flurry of thoughts racing through my head, I'm afraid all that came out of my mouth was a nervous laugh (it was either that or a bit of sick) as I bolted for the exit and left my mother to fend for herself with her new best friends. When I caught up with her later, even more disturbingly, she was rather flattered by the whole exchange!

'It makes a change from being mistaken for Michael's daughter.' All in all, a chilling sauna experience. Lesson learnt: always read the signs! They should probably add some more: 'You use the sauna at your own risk if you are pregnant, or if you ever have been pregnant with the person accompanying you.'

Not surprisingly, my father is less open-minded when it comes to being at one with nature. For him, loosening his tie and undoing the top button of his shirt feels slightly sordid, as if the world is salivating desperately for an eyeful of his hirsute moob-cleavage and he's simply not going to give it the satisfaction. Indeed, I remember the struggle we had getting him to appear without his suit jacket on when we first started shooting *Travels with My Father*. It was in Thailand and he was to spend the day with me in a kayak

in the baking heat. I pointed out that not only would he be uncomfortably hot if he kept it on, but he would also have to get a life jacket on over the suit: quite an important detail given that, as I may have mentioned before, he can't swim.

'I'm not being seen on screen in my shirtsleeves; it's unbecoming.'

This is a man who genuinely would rather drown than have the world see a glimpse of his forearms. It took hours of producers trying to put his mind at ease (one of them asked if he was worried about a tattoo – that went down well) and even a long-distance FaceTime call with my mother to talk him round. Begrudgingly, he agreed, provided the entire scene was filmed in a long shot. The fact that four years later, in Australia, I had him in a gay bar on stage performing a drag show in tights and a pink dress is testament to quite how much I have broken his spirit down over the ensuing years. But it has been an arduous process – like the sea eroding Norfolk; it doesn't happen overnight. Helping him become more comfortable around human flesh has been one of the biggest hurdles.

Naked yoga was my first attempt – and the phrase 'walk before you can run' springs to mind, or in this case 'before you can bow'. As if getting him to agree to do yoga in the first place hadn't, in itself, been enough of a struggle.

'I'll come and assess it myself, but I'm not wearing Lycra!'

'Oh, don't worry, Daddy, if there's one thing I can guarantee about this experience, I promise you no one will be wearing Lycra.'

With the benefit of hindsight, what I probably should have done is take on each element separately. Maybe I should first have arranged a yoga class at the Garrick Club with some of the members, none of them having to take off their tweed

suits, some copies of the *Sunday Times* rolled out on the floor where the mats would be, the scented candles replaced with a waft of cigar smoke and bigotry. Perhaps putting on something relaxing for them in the background, like a marching band or Laurence Fox reading an SAS memoir: creating a nice familiar atmosphere to put him at ease and help him take the leap of faith. Though, in all honesty, I'm not sure how successful a class there might be, telling a couple of geriatric Tory backbenchers and the only living cast member of *Last of the Summer Wine* to assume the downward-facing dog, waiting for the cloud of talcum powder and dandruff to settle, only to realise that none of the participants were ever getting up from the pose.

Equally, getting Daddy to appreciate naturalism – or is it naturism? I can never remember which one is which, which has, on occasion, resulted in me having a very disturbing mental image of Bill Oddie in my head . . . Anyway, whichever one means taking your clothes off. As I say, getting Daddy to appreciate naturism, I might have been better served picking an activity that he was already au fait with: naked Scrabble, nude bridge, croquet in the buff. But yoga and nudity at the same time? I realised pretty quickly that I had bitten off more than I could chew.

'Clothes are our armour, Mike,' Nathan, our naked yoga instructor, explained to my father in his soothing tones. 'We wear them to protect ourselves, but this is a safe space. You have nothing to fear.'

At least I think that's what he said. To be honest with you, he was stark-bollock naked and my attention had drifted elsewhere. Sir Michael Caine again: it's very hard to pay attention to the actual content of what someone's saying when they

aren't wearing any clothes. I swear, politicians would be able to get away with a lot more if they realised this. Boris could have a field day if he did PMQs in his birthday suit. We'd probably never ask him anything again. God, can you imagine? I bet he'd look like a snowman made of sausage meat and straw? Human andouillette. Anyway, Daddy had certainly not heard a word of what Nathan had said as, before the sentence was even out of his mouth, Michael was out of the door.

'No way!'

As the other members of our class peeled off their tie-dye T-shirts and loosened up, it was left to me to convince Daddy that he might learn something from the experience.

'The whole purpose of our travelling together is that you try new things.'

This is my go-to argument for when he's at his most recalcitrant. And it's one you can use on your own parents to guilt-trip them into most things. There followed a tricky negotiation in which he finally agreed he would take off his waistcoat and watch. Waistcoatless yoga.

I think it's safe to say that my father did not leave naked yoga totally converted, and I'm not going to lie, I had some reservations myself. The tense discussion we had outside meant that, unfortunately, we were the last to join the class. In turn, that meant we were last to pick our mats. The resounding lesson I came away with that day is that if you are doing naked yoga, whatever you do, make sure you get a spot at the front. That is not a class you want to be stuck at the back for. Trying to empty your mind and enter a Zen state is hard enough as it is. It's made even more difficult when you have four blokes in front of you bending over to assume the Goddess Twist. People tell you the Niagara Falls is a sight that

will take your breath away, but they don't know what they're talking about. At one point, I think I saw internal organs. It also didn't help that we were in California, where I think the level of manscaping and self-care exceeds anywhere else in the world. I started to feel very insecure about my unkempt physique. The man directly in front of me looked like he'd been carved by Michelangelo and was waxed and bleached to within an inch of his life. Every time he bent over, it was like opening a fridge door. It lit up the room. And the glutes! You could have parked a bike in there! My insecurities were also not helped by my father's insistence on spending the entire session heckling me. As the whole class low-lunged in unison, him pointing out that I was the only person in the class not touching the floor was not called for.

It's also one of those experiences that is fun at the time but one that you forget will be committed to film and then pumped out on Netflix around the globe. It's nice feeling you have international reach, but it also means there are people in Kuala Lumpur who have laughed at your bum. This was a reality that caught me off guard when I stayed at a hotel in Upstate New York some months after the show had aired. The lady at reception could barely contain her amusement as she checked me out of my room. I initially assumed this was because the pay-TV channels had shown up on my itemised bill, but it wasn't that.

She whispered mischievously as she handed me my bill, 'I've been watching you doing your naked yoga.'

I, of course, knew to what she was referring. Unfortunately, the couple checking in next to me did not. They must have thought that I not only had rather an unusual pastime, but that the rooms in this hotel were perhaps not quite as private as the

brochure had boasted. 'Which room would you like, sir?' the gentleman was asked. *Not that guy's*, I could see him thinking.

So, while I'm still very much a 'yes man', there are definitely some caveats. There may come a time in your life when you are confronted with activities that purport to require clothing as only an option. My advice is: if you are with your parents, choose the option to wear them. Clothes are the armour you do not want to forgo!

Hilary's Top 10 Mothers' Travel Dos and Don'ts

1. **DO think before you stop:** Stopping at motorway service stations with children requires as much planning as a short-distance house move or a medium-sized royal wedding. If you have to break your journey for any reason, make sure you pick the service station with the least retail opportunities you can find: ideally a toilet and a kiosk selling petrol. There's nothing worse than pulling over for a quick wee and finding you've stopped at the BP garage that appears to have a Westfield attached to it. Or, even worse, an amusement arcade. Nothing will hold up a journey as much as having to explain to your children why a fruit machine has nothing to do with their five-a-day (as Michael is liable to point out, you should probably be able to tell that from the state of the people using it). If in doubt, opt for the lay-by and a bush. Far rather have them bringing mud back into the car than the entire Ginsters range and a hitchhiker.

2. **DO NOT give the kids their pocket money early:** If you hand over your children's holiday pocket money at the airport, it will all be spent long before you even get within sight of the departure gate. You may think you are giving them a salutary lesson in fiscal responsibility, but the end result will be your son in a sulk for a day because he blew his entire allowance entering a raffle for a sports car he doesn't even possess a licence to drive!

3. **DO NOT accept 'livestock' from strangers:** I was once handed two live crabs in a carrier bag as a treat to take home from Cornwall (it seemed like a nice gesture, but looking back it may have been the locals taking some form of revenge for our stay). The minute we hit the motorway, they escaped and proceeded to terrify the children and razz up the dog, who barked at them all the way back to London as they crawled around the back of the car. If you think I'm the only one to make this mistake, think again. Michael told me that Jack brought crabs back from his 'lads' trip' to Prague, which is strange as I thought the Czech Republic was landlocked.

4. **DO take carrier bags everywhere:** Never embark on any motorway trip without being fully prepared for a child acquainting you with the contents of their guts. They use long-distance driving as a natural emetic, similar to the way cats eat grass. I once had the misfortune to misplace the all-important carrier bag and the only thing I could think to use as Molly started to retch was my outstretched hands. I then had the unenviable task of cradling her vomit all the way to the next service station, whilst trying to prevent the dog from trying to eat it.

Just carry plenty of receptacles, about a mile of loo roll and Smints. And make sure none of these items are buried underneath the luggage in the boot. They're of no use there when you're trundling along at 70mph and your ashen-faced child locks eyes with you in the rear-view mirror and says, 'I think I'm going to be sick!' Your lack of foresight may result in an impromptu green arrows air display from the sun roof or, as happened to Michael on one disastrous occasion, a wellington boot being written off. Also be *very* careful with what snacks you allow them to consume. All vibrant colours or strong odours should be avoided. It's all very well tasting the rainbow, but you're the one who's going to have to scrape it off the back seats of the Volvo when your child has pebble-dashed it with a family bag of regurgitated Skittles.

5. **DO confiscate with care:** It is never a good idea to confiscate electronic devices before any kind of holiday travel. You will be doing yourself no favours at all, however big the misdemeanour. Weigh up the useful disciplinary effect of the punishment against the reality of enduring your child's distraction-free company – it's never worth it. At home, it's best to limit their time on the iPad; on a long-haul flight, handcuff them to it!

6. **DO check children for unwanted cargo:** Nits were the scourge of our entire family. I say entire family: Mr Whitehall swerved them. His theory was his hair was so thin they couldn't get a proper grip. I think they took one taste of his blood and realised they couldn't survive on something that was 80 per cent proof. No holiday was complete without the discovery of nits, thereby

necessitating never-ending evenings of applying noxious, oily treatments and doing battle with my faithful nit comb. I seriously considered taking the children to the hairdressers to get their heads wet-shaved, but my lovely hairdresser, Timothy Williams in Barnes, refused to cut their hair during an infestation. This is the case with virtually all hairdressers, but I am not one to be put off lightly. I considered putting out feelers to some sheep shearers who fancied a bit of extra cash-in-hand, but eventually managed to find the one barber in Putney who was not so scrupulous. Admittedly his shop was a little crude and had the look of a place that might have a few cash-flow issues, so I assumed he was happy with any kind of business. Michael remarked that it had the air of the Sweeney Todds about it and Jack swore blind that he once saw a chunk of ear lobe on the floor among the hair clippings. As ever, he was overreacting, but to be fair to Jack, the barber was the wrong side of seventy, wore thick pebble glasses and had the hint of a tremor. Still, any port in a storm. I was relieved when he finally swept up all the infested hair (at least the portion of it that wasn't able to crawl away of its own volition) and disposed of it for us.

I have already probably been more indiscreet than I should and, at the risk of embarrassing my children even further, there was even one dreadful holiday when I had to contend not only with nits but also with some critters who had decided to let themselves in via the tradesman's entrance. A fresh hell, scraping their heads (and mine) for nit eggs, while at the same time trying to deworm them with anthelmintic cream. A battle at both ends!

7. **DO wash thoroughly:** Always use a lead when taking the family dog for its pre-journey wee-wee walk (to be honest, it's tempting to do the same with a toddler). This will prevent having to bath your pooch just as you are leaving because it's rolled in fox poo. Not only is this time-consuming, you'll also want to avoid a long journey with a damp, steaming dog in the car. For the same reason, all children's outdoor sports should be banned for several hours before departure. Hungover teenagers should be given a careful once-over and maybe even a precautionary coating of Febreze before being allowed into the vehicle. In fact, the only time a hot wet dog can be useful in a car is if you are using it to mask the smell of a teenage son who's idea of personal hygiene extends to a squirt of Lynx Africa down his trousers once a month. The lesser of two evils.

8. **DO get ahead of schoolwork:** As your children grow up, exam boards begin to dictate your holidays, even the destinations. Your entire lifestyle is the product of the whims of Edexcel. The five-star hotel in Barbados you visited as a carefree young couple is traded for a campsite in Lancashire that just happens to be next to an oxbow lake. Onerous holiday art projects will not only clog up all your luggage with endless equipment, but also literally consume your every waking hour. So get them done early. This will avoid any last-minute horror stories the evening before the return to school, when it is discovered that a twenty-page project on castles, complete with illustrations and photographic evidence, needs to be handed in first lesson on Monday morning. The other

killer is the holiday diary, not just because it has to be completed every day for weeks but also because, as a parent, there is an onus on you to make sure that your little darlings' days are packed full of edifying activities to write about. I imagine Samuel Pepys's mum had much the same anxieties. I had sleepless nights about the prospect of one of my children being picked by the teacher to read their diary aloud, and my parenting being put on trial. The whole thing could turn out to be a dossier of incriminating evidence, ready to be passed directly to social services. The saintly and affluent Reynolds boy in Jack's year regaling the class with tales of his summer spent on safari, doing a little conservation work, then spending his evenings stargazing and brushing up on his Swahili, only to be followed by Jack getting up and reading out his diary in which every entry was: 'Got up, had breakfast, played Nintendo, had lunch, watched TV, did a poo, had supper, watched more TV, went to bed.' Oh, the shame. My advice is to take a little creative licence with these diary entries. I made sure that there was plenty of flesh on the bones of the children's recollection of their holidays, even if that meant that their diaries could quite legitimately be considered for the Booker Prize, certainly meeting the threshold for being categorised as works of fiction. The pages of Jack's would be peppered with accounts of fantastical trips to Glyndebourne and the RSC (including at one point a colourful and completely invented account of him being talent-spotted by Sir Trevor Nunn). Molly would be subtly encouraged to write about the cello recital she performed at Christmas, with a cello that had in reality been in the attic for several months

collecting a thick layer of dust and some cobwebs. While Barnaby's offering would include paragraphs about all the books he had delighted in reading over the break, when in truth the only thing I ever saw him browsing was the instruction manual for his Game Boy.

9. **DO pack for all eventualities:** If any member of the family wears contact lenses (random example, let's say a son), make sure that you pack an extra set to cover the duration of the holiday. Failing that, pack a back-up pair of glasses for them, even if they don't like wearing them because it makes them look like Sue Perkins. Ditto prescription drugs for chronic conditions. For instance, if one of your family suffers from, say (again a random example), intermittent bouts of gout, make sure they are travelling with enough medication to alleviate any attacks. The worst holiday was when both of these eventualities happened simultaneously on a late Saturday afternoon of a bank holiday weekend. It was left to me to navigate our way through the local town to find an open pharmacy and an optician, while propping up a hopping husband with his hand on one of my shoulders and a blind son leaning on the other. We hobbled along in a line looking like we were in that John Singer Sargent First World War painting *Gassed*.

10. **DO NOT lose the hire car keys:** All car hire companies will only ever give you one key for your rental as part of the web of extortion and scammery by which they make their money. Guard it with your life. I once lost track of the one and only car key on the last day of our holiday in Provence, when we were due to leave that afternoon for the one-hour drive to Avignon to catch the Eurostar

home. A quick call to the car hire company ascertained that the only other key for the car was in Paris and would need to be couriered down to Avignon. I swear I could hear the gleeful rubbing of hands and the popping of champagne corks in the background of the call.

This news resulted in the following series of events: an exhaustive search through the roadside dustbins while Jack made a number of unhelpful remarks to passers-by about how I was 'turning freegan'; our luggage having to be decanted into the van of a very helpful local farmer who had kindly agreed to drive us to the station; the car having to be abandoned in the villa's driveway, meaning that the next residents had to navigate their way around it; an extra two-week charge for the car, as the key was obviously trans-ported from Paris by carrier pigeon; and many, many tears.

The embarrassing footnote to this story is that, a week after our return to London, I found said key in the bottom of a carrier bag of Provençal soap I'd bought from a market. I was left with a moral dilemma: admit the guilty secret to my family or leave them in blissful ignorance? In the end, I opted for the latter. This is the first time I've revealed the truth about the car key to the world, so a bit of a scoop for the book.

Rest and recuperation are the main objectives of getting away. And if you can't find peace in naked yoga or a trip to a nude sauna with your own mother, you may have to look for it else-where. Most hotels will try to entice you in with a wide variety of 'treatments' on offer, from facials to foot rubs – obviously one to swerve if you're travelling with old gouty. The most

popular therapy, though, tends to be the massage; nothing de-stresses people more than being face down on a hard treatment bed as a stranger marinades you in oil and tries to find your pressure points. You know this is the most popular treatment as whenever you call up to book one at the hotel you are immediately told by the concierge that the next available spot is seven o'clock on Friday morning of the week after you've returned home. If you weren't feeling stressed before, you will do after you've had an argument down the phone in which you agitatedly explain to the concierge that had you known there were no massages available you might not have spent a fortune booking a 'spa' hotel in the first place. Still, first-world problems and all that. For my father, a man who will literally cut people out of his life if they are deemed to linger too long in a handshake, the notion of letting a masseuse loose on him is extremely daunting. Although not nearly as daunting as it might be to the masseuse: my dad's back probably has more knots in it than the National Maritime Museum. There has only ever been one occasion when Michael has been so desperate that he sought another's healing hands. It happened when we were in the Far East, which means the story he's about to share has some extremely dodgy racial stereotypes in it, and even by his standards some of the most deeply questionable passages of dialogue in the entire book.

Michael's CAMBODIAN MASSAGE STORY

After the Khmer Rouge were overthrown in 1979, Cambodians needed a safe and efficient way to move people

and goods around the country, avoiding the estimated six million uncharted landmines – sadly, many still live today (I realise this represents a somewhat heavy-duty start to what will ultimately lead to an enjoyable and light-hearted anecdote, but stick with it, as the Cambodians sensibly didn't with the Khmer Rouge). We actually visited a minefield while there, which was being cleared with the help of some extremely clever rats. They had been trained to walk across the minefields, which they were able to do as they are not heavy enough to trigger them. But they are able to sniff out the explosive in the landmines and mark the spot by scratching the earth. I'll warrant this doesn't sound like it would be chock-full of comedy, but it turned out to have one small piece of comedy gold at its centre, as the man in charge of the clearance programme who actually took Jack out into the minefield had a first name that was also an instruction. Unbelievably his name was Turn, not a good name to have shouted around when you spend your days carefully navigating active minefields. Still, it could have been worse: I guess he could have been called Stamp.

I digress, also something you're very unwise to do in a minefield. Very few trains currently ran, but the tracks were still in place, so they salvaged old train-carriage wheels and built iron frames on which they laid a platform of bamboo. The platforms, known as Bamboo Trains, moved along the single tracks powered by small motors. The whole thing was only slightly less antiquated and shambolic than Southern railways. There were right-of-way issues, the rule of thumb being that whoever had the most passengers could stay on the track while the oncoming train was dismantled and removed, so there were often disputes about numbers, with

any livestock being included in the headcounts. This meant any impasse quickly escalated to a shouting match from train to train with a lot of angry gesticulation and waving around of chickens.

We spent a hot morning filming for the first series of *Travels with My Father* on the train, sharing its small platform with cameras, while a drone filmed us from the sky. Predictably, for a complicated set-up involving drones, the filming ran on well into the blazing heat of the midday sun. By the time we got back to our hotel in Battambang, I was well and truly knackered and aching all over, having been bounced along the track for hours. I'm not saying it was as bad as some of the things the victims of the Khmer Rouge were subjected to, but it was certainly yet another chapter in Cambodia's long history of visiting suffering upon the nobly innocent.

Later that night, we had dinner with our crew, and one of them helpfully suggested that I had a massage the following day, which happened to be our day off. He did, however, warn me that when booking it at the hotel reception, I should make it clear that I didn't require a happy ending.

'A happy what?' I asked him, not familiar with the term other than in the context of fairy tales and business negotiations.

He explained that it was a service performed at the end of a massage that would have made Mrs Whitehall decidedly unhappy. It was something he had learnt by bitter experience, when trying to extricate himself from such a misunderstanding, or so he claims . . .

'Don't worry, Nick, your secrets are safe with me.' (A promise I have honoured to this day, other than reprinting them in a widely available book.)

The conversation had spooked me. So not only did I make it very clear at the reception that I would be content with a sad ending, even a tragic one – I was perfectly happy with the massage equivalent of the final scene of *Hamlet*, corpses strewn hither and thither – but I also insisted that Jack stay in the room with me during the massage, just to ensure that there was no hanky-panky. I was so out of my comfort zone, having been brought up a strict Catholic in the nineteen-forties and -fifties, by parents who *never* showed an inch of flesh more than they had to and who had sent me away to boarding school when I was ten. Mind you, if I survived that – and the idea of sending a child to a boys' boarding school to protect him from the sins of the flesh seems, in a typically Catholic fashion, to be one based more on faith than logic – I could survive a forty-five-minute massage with a Cambodian lady. And I had the safety net of Jack as a chaperone, sat in the corner of the room like a guard policing a prison visit, on hand to make sure my masseuse didn't get caught up in the moment.

The following afternoon, we awaited the arrival of the masseuse, Jack and I on the bed, him on his computer and me tensing up at the prospect of a sultry young girl arriving at my door and me having to explain to her that I had had an exhausting day on the Bamboo Train (already there was a danger of euphemisms being misunderstood) and just needed a gentle massage to ease my aches and pains. Jack, of course, thought that the whole thing was an enormous joke and threatened to counter my instructions and tell the girl that I was too shy to ask but what I really wanted was a good seeing-to with all the bells and whistles. Not merely a happy ending, but one that would leave me living happily ever after.

There was a knock at the door. Jack started giggling and I told him to shut the fuck up (you can't put a price on this sort of father–son rapport) and get back to the script he was writing on his computer. I opened the door to be greeted by the maid armed with a bucket and small Hoover. A short, portly lady of a certain age, with precious little English and what sounded to me like the beginnings of a nasty cough.

'You Whyhole?' she asked.

'Yes,' I replied. 'Could you come back later? I'm working with my son at the moment.'

'No, must do you now,' she said, a little too aggressively, I thought. She was clearly a woman with a personality as strong as her very visible forearms. I paused for thought. 'Me Bopha,' she added.

Unfortunately I misheard her last remark as 'me bonker'.

'No, madam, I am really not interested in that, thank you. I'm waiting for a massage, so I'm afraid you have to come and clean later.'

'No!' she exclaimed. 'Me Bopha, massage. I have more client in one hour, I must do you now.'

'Oh my God,' I thought to myself. *She* was the masseuse. 'Must do you now' – this was not the language of a relaxing spa. In fact, it had more of a feel of Kwik Fit. She headed off to the bathroom to 'change', and thankfully returned fully dressed in a white smock. She emptied her bucket of products and asked me to remove my dressing gown, which I did with no great enthusiasm.

'Easy, Mike,' giggled Jack, who was being of no help whatsoever. He later described me as undressing 'like a bashful virgin', which I don't think gives a remotely accurate picture.

Bopha proceeded to put me on my front and sit on my

back, her thighs either side of my neck. It was like being in a nutcracker made of flesh. I thought I was going to suffocate, such was the weight on my back, and I was pinned in a full neck lock, a million miles away from anything that could even loosely be described as hanky-panky. My member had retreated so far up my abdomen, it could have been mistaken for an intellectual in hiding from Pol Pot. She then began to pummel and prod me in a pretty unforgiving manner, and I was certainly not feeling in any way relaxed. It was only when she released me from her entwining thighs that I realised that the shaking of the bed, which I thought had been caused by the bopping from Bopha, was in fact caused by Jack trying unsuccessfully to stifle his hysterical laughter.

Bopha asked me to turn onto my back as she wanted to rub in some healing ointments. This was too much for Jack, who sprang off the bed.

'I need the bathroom,' he managed to blurt out through his sniggers.

'Well, don't be too long,' I implored him. 'I don't want to be left unchaperoned a second longer than I have to,' I said as Bopha began to straddle me again with her ample thighs.

'You'll be fine; Bopha has got this covered,' he managed to get out through his guffaws.

'Yes, that's what I am worried about!' I retorted as he shut the bathroom door. I hoped to God he wasn't going to find a camera.

Bopha applied the foul-smelling and very sticky medicinal emollient and began to rub it vigorously all over my body. Suddenly the vapours must have caught her in the back of her throat, causing her hacking cough to explode and over-whelm both her and me. She leapt off me, waved her arms

around and headed for the bathroom, which fortunately Jack was just vacating, having regained his composure. She locked the door and continued to cough for several minutes, as Jack reverted back to being helpless with laughter.

On her return, she began to straddle me again to resume the oiling process. I felt I was being less massaged, more prepared for a cross-Channel swim. As she worked away on me, Jack could no longer resist the temptation to get involved.

'You've missed a bit,' he said to her, with a huge grin on his face, pointing to my nether regions. Bopha smirked, now in on the joke and as amused as Jack by my discomfort. It was time to tap out.

'Thank you so much,' I said as I grabbed my dressing gown, 'but I feel so relaxed now that I don't think I need any more of your magic touch. But that was most enjoyable.' She gathered up her equipment and there was a slight tinge of regret that I never found out what she did with the contraption that looked like a mini Hoover (it didn't seem like the kind of thing to create a happy ending, more a bloody denouement) but I definitely didn't want to delay her departure any more than I had to. And I certainly didn't want to give Jack any more comedy ammunition. I thought some kind parting words were the least she deserved after the intense physical journey we'd been on together, so as I walked her to the door I said, 'I'd get that cough looked at by a doctor if I were you.'

When I went down for dinner later that evening, the receptionist called me over and handed me the masseuse's card and her bill.

'She left you her card in case you needed a follow-up visit. She said how nice you both were.'

'How sweet of her,' I said to Jack as we walked off, while inwardly thinking her analysis could only be the result of the language barrier. I glanced at the bill and realised that her kind appraisal of our characters was clearly to soften the blow of charging us for a couples' massage. I can only hope she didn't think Jack and I were in a romantic relationship – Hilary may enjoy that sort of misunderstanding, but I don't want even a complete stranger to think I have such low standards.

Cultural Etiquette

THIS NEXT CHAPTER IS particularly pertinent given what you've just read. It's all about respecting other people's cultures. I kind of wish I'd written it a decade ago and had it tattooed to the inside of Daddy's eyelids.

Every part of the world has its own cultural customs. Even Yorkshire. Whether they be silly social quirks or strict religious decrees, all are potential banana skins for the considerate holidaymaker. Unfortunately, when it comes to your family, the 'considerate' element cannot be taken for granted; actually, mine are pretty considerate, it's just that the main thing they consider is themselves. Sadly a lot of British tourists can be a little bit blasé about all of this, seeing these cultural customs more as casual suggestions rather than strict laws. I think it's probably a latent colonial superiority woven into our DNA. Our ancestors came over here, shot a few locals and forced anyone still standing to

build them nice houses and play cricket. Now, hundreds of years and a few revolutions later, we must fight the urge to blunder back into these countries, slapping the natives on the back, demanding milk in our tea and wearing our hats wherever we please.

For older generations of your family who seem the least consumed with fear of upsetting the locals, it's worth reminding them just how perturbed *they* get when British cultural customs aren't adhered to by our visitors. In London, for example, a city where smiling at a stranger is seen as an act of hostility (the equivalent in many other countries of pulling a gun), they might have witnessed that awful moment when a tourist tries to start a conversation with a commuter on the Tube! The whole carriage looking at the American in disgust (it *could* be another nationality, sure, but let's face it, it's likely to be an American). A whole Tube carriage can nearly be derailed by the collective eye-rolling.

Let's face it, we don't like it when the boot is on the other foot. Or, for that matter, when the boot is not on the foot at all. Imagine, if you will, the chorus of dismay were a Johnny Foreigner to turn up at Sunday mass in open-toe sandals (even though I can't imagine that Jesus himself would have turned up in a pair of brogues). Blasphemy! Sacrilege! And any Brit who thinks it's a bit of an overreaction when Italians get uppity because we've ordered a cappuccino after dinner should try to remember quite how enraged they became that time they saw a group of Italian teenagers at Waterloo station trying to join a queue en masse from the side. I'm not having a pop at Italians; I love Italy. It is an enlightened nation in terms of art, music, fashion, cuisine. But when it comes to queuing, they are in the Dark Ages.

Maybe it's all karma for the behaviour of the Brits abroad. Tit-for-tat warfare. In Japan, it's rude to point at people or to blow your nose in public. Many's the British tourist I saw in Tokyo violating these sacred customs. Maybe that's why, when Japanese tourists come to England, they like standing on the wrong side of escalators. I'm not saying it's necessarily a national conspiracy, with the whole of Japan so gravely insulted by having grubby Benson-and-Hedges-stained fingers thrust towards them that they have collectively decided to wreak havoc on Britain's public transport system for generations to come, like some incredibly slow-burning Pearl Harbor. And dare I add how perturbed some Brits used to be at the sight of Japanese tourists walking around London in those ridiculous masks.

'That may be part of your culture but it isn't over here, mate! The Queen's smoggy, carbon-riddled, pea-soup air not good enough for you, is it? Breathing in our mix of diesel particulates and other people's mucus discharge not to your liking? Why don't you take off that mask? Or if you don't want to adhere to our culture, head back to Mount Fuji! Mark my words, those masks will never take off in Great Britain!'

Yeah, had to back-pedal on that one, didn't we? Turns out, they may have had a point. Oops.

I think the most important lesson is a really simple one: treat others' homes with the same respect you'd like them to treat yours.

With some of these cultural dos and don'ts, it's simply about kicking old habits. For example, in Britain there is a funny little idiosyncrasy, something we all do. It transcends class,

age and gender. If a British person is in a pub or restaurant – any public place, for that matter – and they hear the sound of a glass smashing, they will leap up and go, 'Whey!' It's burnt into us like the fight-or-flight response. Whether it be a primary-school kid hearing a juice box connect with the floor of the canteen or a little old lady in a care home hearing a cup of water smashing and a set of dentures hitting the carpet, we cannot help ourselves. It's in our very nature, ingrained in us from birth, a knee-jerk reaction: you hear someone drop something, you cheer. I suspect it's because, for British people, nothing is more worth celebrating than someone else's misery. It turns out, that's not something they do in America. Well, no one told me that when I went there, did they?! I cheered a smash in America and it did not go down well. It wasn't my fault. I heard a crash, I jumped up and went, 'Whey!' The filthy looks that I got. Anyone would have thought *I* had dropped that coffin.

OK, thankfully it wasn't a coffin, but it may as well have been for the reaction I got from the waiters. Yes, it turns out in other countries they don't want to draw attention to other people's misfortune and share collective delight in it, but would rather offer pity or assistance. Bizarre. It'll never catch on. But a valuable lesson learnt and one I can now pass on to you: if you hear a glass smash on holiday, keep calm, carry on, don't cheer. Unless you're in Greece, where they actively encourage that sort of thing. They love getting smashy with the crockery. Every wedding is like an episode of *ChuckleVision*. Still, I say that the plate-smashing tradition in Greece is definitely one you need to double-check is a thing at the place where you're dining at before you join in. I got very drunk once in Mykonos and managed to convince

my friend Hugo (of course he was called Hugo), who was even more lit than me, that the restaurant we were in, which I think turned out to be a French bistro, was famous for letting you smash your plate on the floor at the end of the meal. Hugo, who is pretty gullible even when sober, duly obliged and our whole party was ejected from the premises for vandalising their property. An excellent prank you could play on a gullible family member if you want to curtail an otherwise boring meal.

Something that I want to make clear is that if you do mess up, it really isn't the end of the world. I don't want to strike fear into your heart with any of these warnings. Often it's the case that the cultural custom you are warned about is something you wouldn't dream of doing in the first place. Thailand has a fair few of these. You mustn't point with your feet. Good to know. I'll have to try out these weird prongs at the end of my arms then, I guess. Always wondered what they were for. Never had any use for them before but there's a first time for everything.

There's also the instruction that my father and I were given upon arriving at our first Buddhist temple in Bangkok.

'As we enter this temple I must remind you of one very important rule,' our guide Pru told us in hushed tones. 'You are not allowed to touch a monk on the head.'

Come again? It kind of worried me that that was even a rule they felt they had to tell people. What was happening before? Were tourists putting monks in headlocks? Spotting dull-headed ones and giving the old bonce a quick spit and polish? Maybe these guides imagine it's the sort of thing we're always getting up to back home – as if a British Sunday isn't complete without a trip to an abbey to happy-slap an

entire Benedictine order or bash a bishop. For the love of God, even the most idiotic tourist must know not to touch a monk's head in a temple, or anyone's for that matter. Surely, the type of person that succumbs to impulses like that doesn't even get onto the plane. That person's been detained at customs for grabbing the policeman's gun. In fact, *that's* the guy who takes the crossbow or fireworks in his hand luggage. The annoying thing about the way my brain works is that I honestly, hand on heart, wouldn't have dreamt of touching a monk's head but, from the minute I was told that I shouldn't, every time I saw one, there was a voice in my head going, 'Touch it, touch it, touch it.'

My father was less fazed, having spent most of his youth around monks at his Catholic boarding school, Ampleforth.

'I was brought up to respect monks; I don't need instructions on how to behave around them.'

All right, monk whisperer.

'In fact, at my school, you had to be more worried about the monks touching you.'

'Please, don't translate that, Pru.' This became somewhat of a catchphrase of mine when we were in Thailand.

For my father, the custom that shoes had to be taken off when entering places was a cause of endless frustration in the Far East. He'd always try to argue the point, as if thousands of years of tradition can be negotiated away like a billing dispute with the producers of *Rumpole of the Bailey*. He's never been one for unnecessary de-shoeing, especially at airport security. I always remember the time my mum got new carpets and tried to change our house into a shoes-off-at-the-front-door residence. My dad was having none of it and, during one tense confrontation at the threshold, as

my mother tried to wrestle him out of his brogues, came out with the immortal line: 'Hilary, this is a home not a mosque!'

In Thailand he attempted to circumnavigate the no-shoes-indoors policy by getting our guide Pru to tell everyone that he suffered from gout, which could in rare instances be highly contagious (in fact, gout is only contagious if someone else with gout feeds you port and cheese for thirty years). It was like a teenage girl trying to get out of swimming with lady problems.

Upon travelling to some regions, you will hear a fair amount of scaremongering before you go. If you're off to Dubai, for example, there's always that one friend, who you suspect has never actually been, that wants to fill your head with horror stories. You'll have just told him where you're going in the pub and he'll put down his pint gravely and be like . . .

'Did you know . . .'

Here we go.

'. . . that in Dubai it is illegal to walk through a shopping mall naked?'

'Right, Steve, I'm pretty sure that's illegal in England as well.'

'They'll arrest you for it. Give you a fine.'

'Mate, honestly, try that in Harvey Nichols. See if no one complains.'

'And you can go to prison for eating on public transport.'

Can you, though? I mean, I'm sure it's frowned upon, might even be illegal, but you think they have many incarcerations for it? It would be a really bad crime to end up in jail for. Quite an awkward first day in the clink, when you're settling down for night one of your ten stretch in a maximum-security wing, having a little idle pillow talk with your new cellmate.

'So, Hussein, what are you in here for?'

'I went on a killing spree, murdering fifteen people with my bare hands, slowly crushing their skulls with my fingers, watching the life drain from their eyes until their heads were a pulp, then I cut up their bodies and made trophies out of their genitals. What about you?'

'I ate a Kinder Bueno on the monorail.'

Look, it's definitely worth being aware of these laws, but I'd like to see the crime statistics for just how many people in Singapore actually get imprisoned for chewing-gum-related crimes. I suspect there are fewer people than you might expect on the Wrigley's wing.

A lot of the mishaps in Asia tend to involve the hands and feet. In India, you're meant to eat with your right hand and wipe your bum with the left. I was terrified, when I went, that I'd mix them up. So I played it safe and brought a spork and used that instead. Although I did have to stop after a while as it was really beginning to hurt my arse. How do you think I got that rash? The 'one for bum, one for tum' system means that offering your left hand to shake another person's – or to do anything else with, for that matter – really can be a bit of a no-no. On the whole, it's best to keep your hands to yourself. In Iraq, that is quite literally a rule of thumb, as putting said digit up to someone is considered a very offensive gesture. If you haven't been made aware of that, you could get into some very sticky situations in the region, especially if you're hitchhiking. There must have been backpackers who stood at the side of the road for days in Iraq wondering why no one had stopped to pick them up, only to discover they've been accidently telling the passing vehicles to go fuck themselves. In Vietnam crossing your

fingers is equally obscene. It's a gesture that represents the female genitalia. I got told that by our fixer in Hanoi. He'd spotted my father doing the gesture every time he asked to see a wine list. Obviously, I didn't tell him, hoping that eventually we'd find a restaurant that misinterpreted his request and brought out something fruity and full-bodied from the cellar. In Spain, it's the 'rock on' gesture that could raise a few eyebrows. Raising your index and pinkie fingers at another man infers the cuckold's horns – that is, that the man in question's wife has been unfaithful. It's a sure-fire way to sour the atmosphere of even the most buoyant mosh pit. Probably why they mainly stick to flamenco. In general, my advice is to be on the safe side and maybe just keep your hands in your pockets. Oh, unless you're in South Korea, where that's also deemed extremely offensive.

Most of the mistakes you might make abroad are less criminal acts or grave insults and more run-of-the-mill, everyday social faux pas. The perfect example of this is greetings. From handshakes to high-fives, all cultures have different ways of greeting one another. Malaysians put their hands together on their hearts. In Tibet, you stick out your tongue. If you're travelling in Japan, remember to sheathe your handshake in favour of a bow when you're addressing someone older than you, of higher social status or just really short. And if you're white, please avoid fist bumps wherever you are, whatever the circumstances. They are never acceptable, ever. You won't look gangsta, you'll look like a toddler playing 'one potato, two potato'. Europeans, of course, are fairly tactile. We tend to favour the air kiss from cheek to cheek, a custom that originated in ancient Rome, where else? Those frisky Romans probably cooked

it up over a game of slap-and-tickle in the Thermae. It's so common a greeting on the Continent that I once heard an American rather unnervingly refer to it as 'French kissing', which I had to inform him meant something very different indeed. If you greet strangers with a French kiss, you're getting into Weinstein territory. The standard form of the greeting requires no actual lip-to-skin contact at all, but rather confusingly the number of air kisses required on each cheek varies significantly from country to country (the whole thing's an exchange-rate nightmare). Two kisses are required in Spain and in Italy; three if you're in Belgium or Slovenia; in Hungary, they prefer you to plant it on their hand; in Glasgow, the kiss is performed a little differently by driving the top of the forehead into the bridge of the other person's nose – the Glasgow kiss, as it's known. In France, the number of kisses can change from region to region: in snog-happy Nantes, you'd be expected to serve up three, but down the road in more reserved Toulouse, it's just the two; whereas if you're giving someone a Brest kiss, best to make it a satisfying one-off, and probably ask the bill-payer's permission first. To make matters even more confusing, while some Europeans love a smooch, others don't go in for it at all, perhaps reasoning that what they lose in intimacy, they gain in reduced staph infections. In the South of France you could be *faire la bise*-ing for up to twenty minutes – I've come back from trips to Provence with whiplash – but if you were to take a short flight to Bulgaria and kiss a man three times on his cheek, he'd most likely give you a black eye for your troubles as theirs is a no-kissing-at-all kind of place.

It's all very confusing. I've always thought that really this is something the EU could have done something about.

Surely that should be one of the advantages of the European bloc, putting an end to this volatile kiss economy. If they can have a common market, couldn't they pass a law in Brussels to have a coherent continent-wide legislation on the number of kisses required when meeting a person? A single air-kiss currency to avoid any further confusion or unwanted amorousness? It's the people of Bulgaria I feel most sorry for.

It isn't just Europe, to be fair. In other parts of the world, you might be required to pucker up too, but usually with a few more ground rules. In Ecuador, cheek kissing tends to be reserved for men only, and a kiss is only required Down Under if you're really good friends. By 'Down Under' I mean 'in Australia'; that probably needs clarification. Now I read that last sentence back, it doesn't quite sound right. Even among the closest Ecuadorians, a kiss down under when greeting might be considered a tad overfamiliar.

Still, how about this for friendly: in some parts of Afghanistan, it's customary to kiss each other up to eight times on each cheek (by 'each' I mean the top two) to say goodbye! No wonder it took the Americans nineteen years to leave.

It's not just what you do with your mouth that could get you in trouble (as we were once told in Sex Ed), but what comes out of it too. Saying the wrong thing when greeting someone abroad can be just as offensive.

Australians have a friendly disposition and it's customary for them to greet you by asking you how things are going. Please don't confuse this with a genuine interest. If an Aussie asks you, 'How's it going, mate?' the accepted response is: 'Good, mate.' Or if you're having a bad day: 'Fine, mate.' Do not let their question deceive you: they don't actually care.

They were just being friendly. Now let them make their way to their barbie.

The Australian, I have found, is pretty much unoffendable. Unless the Australian you have greeted is, in fact, a New Zealander. That's hard to recover from. In fact, that's a really good rule of thumb: if you hear an accent, always go with the little brother nation just to be safe. If you think you can hear an American twang, safer to assume they might be Canadian. An Englishman will never be upset if you think he's Scottish, but if you accuse a Scot of being a lily-livered London luvvie, you could end up on the wrong end of a barrage of insults, only some of which you will be able to understand.

I think the only way you could insult an Australian is by turning up to a gathering empty-handed. A dry guest is an unwelcome one. Which leads me nicely on to the cultural etiquettes surrounding drinking. These are the international drinking rules.

In Australia, if you're invited to any social event, you *must* assume it is BYOB. That's 'bring your own booze'. As opposed to, say, in Saudi Arabia, where you must assume it's BYOBGFIATS. That's 'bring your own booze, get flogged in a town square'.

In some nations, you can cause grave offence by not making eye contact when clinking a glass. In Japan, one is not meant to pour one's own saké. And in some parts of Latin America, pouring a drink with your left hand is considered bad luck, especially if you're pouring it under a ladder while standing on a grave. In LA, drinking with lunch is frowned upon (particularly weird for us Brits, who are probably still sobering up from breakfast and could really do with something to take the edge off).

In France, it is frowned upon to pour yourself a refill of wine before offering it to others first, though it can be hard to tell if you have committed this faux pas, as a lot of the company you keep in France will be frowning as standard. It is, after all, the national resting face, especially when in the company of English people. In South Korea, it is considered rude to ask for a refill of your glass unless it is empty first. Pre-loading and double-parking are also probably not big in Korea. In fact, as was the case with cheering a smashed glass, there are a number of Britain's rather more uncouth drinking traditions that are less prevalent elsewhere: 'down it or wear it', 'the beer hunter', 'pennying', 'mine-sweeping' and 'straight-arming' your pint are not practices commonly recognised on the Continent or anywhere much beyond the four walls and one sticky floor of your regional Tiger Tiger. And, please, don't ask for an Irish car bomb in Ireland. I'm not saying you won't be offered one, especially if you ask with an accent like mine; they may just choose to take your request more literally.

There are more cultural customs than I have space for in these pages and I could go on for days. The Arab world does not appreciate PDAs. I mean, much of the western world doesn't appreciate them either but we just don't have the power to deport you for foisting them upon us. You can't pay with pennies in Canada. No selfies in the red light district of Amsterdam. Though why you'd want to keep a record of what you're getting up to there totally escapes me. In China, it's a faux pas to blow your nose in public or question the authority of the state. And punctuality is held in extremely high regard in both Germany and South Korea, where being late is a sign of disrespect

compared to, say, in America, where it's more than accept-able to turn up to events 'fashionably late': a custom they took to the extreme in attending the Second World War, itself a gathering that the Germans were, alas, if anything a little too punctual for. Oh and that brings me nicely on to the final faux pas: in the words of Basil Fawlty, don't mention the war.

So, do your research and make sure all family members have been fully briefed too. Be aware of the dos and don'ts, the kissers and the shakers. Make sure they're trained in the appropriate ordering of drinks. A little PowerPoint presenta-tion, maybe, in the hotel before letting them loose on the town? Mark my words, you wouldn't want your daughter flashing the flesh in Turkmenistan, your brother crossing his chopsticks in Vietnam or, worst of all, your mother misinterpreting a Nicaraguan man puckering his lips and nodding in the direction of a bush when she's just asked him for directions to the bathroom.

Of course the only sure-fire way to make sure no foreign nationals are upset by your family is to keep the sun cream and your passport locked in the cupboard and instead embark upon a holiday within the British Isles. Feasting on the bountiful spoils that good old Blighty has on offer. Delayed trains, pebble beaches, choking a seagull to death on the remnants of your Cornish pasty, the fun never stops – well, it does at eleven when last orders are called; you're not on the Continent now. Since most of his life was spent holidaying in Britain, bussing around from seaside town to seaside town like Nigel Farage on an election campaign, I shall let Michael muse on the delights of holidaying in your own backyard. If you're near the wireless maybe play some

Edward Elgar as you read it and think to yourself, 'Thank fuck for EasyJet.'

Michael: IT'S NEVER SUNNY IN BOGNOR REGIS

Whenever my children complained about some small imperfection or inconvenience to do with some aspect of one of our holidays, often abroad and always meticulously planned and executed by their super-efficient mother, and usually in a luxury villa or smart hotel, I would remind them that they should count their lucky stars that they hadn't, unlike me, been born in the 1940s, when they would really have had something to complain about.

Margate, Eastbourne, Cromer, Broadstairs, Ramsgate . . . The world was our oyster when it came to family holidays when I was a child, albeit perhaps one of those dodgy oysters that can kill you. After the war, in the late forties, the Whitehall coffers were very depleted and foreign travel way beyond our means. This was decades before the Brits discovered the Costas, Spain still being in the grip of the Fascist dictator Franco; Portugal was not an option because it was under the iron fist of Salazar; and France, alas, even back then was full of the French. So, it was bags packed and off on the train for a week's holiday in a guest house somewhere by the seaside that hadn't been bombed to rubble – sunny Margate or freezing Cromer, where the only weather guarantee was that it would rain at least once every day. This was probably an advantage as far as my parents were concerned, as neither of them enjoyed swimming or sunbathing. My

mother, Nora, was a very shy woman and would never be seen in public unless she was well covered up in several layers. Ideally she would have liked to have had the use of one of those Victorian bathing machines to wheel her down to the water's edge, assuming she could have sourced a long-sleeved, full-length bathing costume, such was her habitual embarrassment and constant fear of being overlooked.

'You've caught the sun,' was a phrase oft used by Nora after a day of sitting on a beach. By 'caught the sun' she meant burnt to a frazzle with a blistered forehead and nose, on which she had dabbed some Nivea cream on arrival in the morning. Although the ancient Egyptians used plants with sun-screening properties, commercially available sunscreens were not really on offer until the sixties, unless you were a rich family vacationing on the Côte d'Azur, which was well out of reach to the Whitehalls. As were smart hotels on the coast, so our accommodation of necessity would be guest houses. These grim places, invariably run for the benefit of the proprietors rather than the guests, would comprise modest bedrooms, with a bathroom shared by all of the residents. There would be a dining room down-stairs, where breakfast was served by the owner, a woman who was often imbued with a wealth of facial hair and a copious bosom, which she would hitch up when she was riled by some contravention of the house rules. Breakfast was an immovable 8 a.m. to 9 a.m. and dinner the same, between 6 p.m. and 7 p.m. The doors of the establishment would be firmly locked throughout the day. The food was terrible and whatever dish the landlady was capable of was usually repeated throughout the week. Breakfast consisted of scrambled egg made with 50 per cent powdered egg and

50 per cent watered-down milk, and dinner would be over-cooked vegetables accompanied by the guest-house plat du jour – Spam. No alcohol was permitted on the premises but smoking was, so the dining area was always shrouded in billowing clouds of smoke, much of it coming from my mother, who would proudly say that she 'didn't inhale', which meant that all of those around her inhaled her smoke! One of these was my saintly father Jack, who sadly as a result developed severe emphysema and ultimately and tragically died well before his time.

As I progressed through my teens in the fifties, my father was earning a bit more and after my maternal grandfather retired to Devon, we migrated further afield with trips down to see him. Paignton and Torquay were now our playgrounds, the latter even having palm trees, which was very exotic even though said palm trees were located on the island of a roundabout next to a Woolworths. Certainly, the landladies down there were an improvement, with less facial hair and marginally better culinary skills. Ultimately, we were able to upscale our accommodation, due to the generosity of my other grandfather, REB Whitehall, and we began to actually stay in hotels.

Romance, of sorts, also entered the fray. On a holiday in Torquay, we met a family staying in the same hotel with two very attractive daughters. My brother Barry made a quick move on the elder of the two and I fell hopelessly in love with the younger one. Time was of the essence, as our holidays were still only ever a week long, despite REB's munificence; the other problem being the constant presence of our parents.

'Sarah's a lovely girl,' Nora would whisper to me, as Sarah

disappeared to the loo. 'You seem very keen on her.' I was indeed, but the problem was that we were in a pub with her sister, my brother, her brother, her parents and my parents. And that particular passion killer remained the case for every evening until we left to go home to London. This was obviously well before the days of the mobile phone, and having been brought up a strict Catholic and sent to a boarding school run by monks from age ten, I was certainly not versed in the ways of the world and was far too shy to ask her for her address or, heaven forbid, phone number. Phone calls in those days had to be made on your parents' phone, which was invariably positioned very publicly in the hall, with three sets of listening ears and the danger that someone other than Sarah might answer it at the other end, and you would need to pluck up the courage to ask to speak to her. No, that was all far too much for me, so I never saw her again, although I did for many years treasure a small black-and-white photo of Barry and me with her and her sister which my mother took on the family Box Brownie camera. The photo was a little blurry unfortunately, not on account of her photography skills, but because at the time of taking it Nora was holding a cigarette, shrouding the whole scene in smoke. That was the nearest I got to romance for many years.

As we got older still, as well as the pub, my father would also treat us all to a trip to see a show at the local variety theatre. Barry and I loved these outings; Nora less so. She felt that they were 'common' and 'not proper theatre', but would grudgingly accompany us nonetheless. I always suspected that she secretly quite enjoyed them but would never let on. There were usually beautiful dancers, a singer, maybe a

magician or a ventriloquist and, my favourite, a comedian. How we all laughed at their corny and inappropriate jokes – well, all of us except Nora, who would always critique any 'comics' as being course and unfunny. Thank God she never lived to see her grandson perform. I think this was my intro-duction to the entertainment business, which I entered ten years later.

So, although considerably more modest than the holidays I managed to treat my own children to, I had nothing to compare them with, so to me they were pretty flawless. They also had the same thing at their heart as the holidays I took my children on: a family bonding exercise that if not always ideal, did at least prove that we could coexist per-fectly happily, if only for a week at a time. And there is a lot of truth in the old adage that a change is as good as a rest, even if the change takes you to a place that is slightly inferior to your own home.

Christmas

THE FAMILY HOLIDAY THAT consumes us more than any other and, thus far, has been glaring by its omission is of course the holiday to end all holidays: Christmas. The annual and, thanks to supermarkets and advertising executives, ever-expanding festival of family oddities, spreading across the calendar like a tumour made of tinsel and unrealistic expectations. Mine is one that is full of archaic traditions and what seem like bizarre and deeply unrelatable family rituals that I will share with you nonetheless. My hope is that we can dig out some hidden lessons from them, even if they are harder to find than that satsuma at the bottom of the stocking. It's a bit like my mother stripping down a turkey carcass: it is not going to be pretty but, hopefully, we can turn the mess into something useful.

Food

And what better place to start than with the turkey? If there's any way of pardoning the turkey from your Christmas plans, I would strongly encourage you to do so. If there is a God – and this is a question I find myself grappling with a lot around that time of year, especially when the calendar ticks round to Boxing Day and I'm still trapped with my family like a hostage wearing a pair of supposedly hilarious novelty antlers – why would he be so cruel as to make the turkey not only the blandest animal on his green and pleasant land, but also such a colossal bastard? One destined to outstay its welcome by dominating your fridge and dragging down every sandwich for weeks. We stuff it with pork, wrap it in bacon, massage butter under its skin, all in a desperate attempt to elevate this scrotum-necked taste-bud dodger. We might as well rip it to bits and stuff it into the walls to serve as cavity insulation. Scientists have even devised ways of inserting other birds within it, double-0 agents of flavour sent deep undercover to rescue this lame excuse for a dinner, a sort of cholesterol-heavy real-life version of that nursery rhyme about the old woman who swallowed a fly. Come to think of it, I suspect it might have been butchers rather than scientists responsible for the Turducken. It would have been a pretty slow day at the lab for them to turn their attention from mRNA cell research to seeing if they could fit a quail inside a duck.

'Hey, guys, how's the COVID vaccine coming along?'

'Yeah, not great, but we did make a poultry Russian doll.'

'You're all fired.'

The reason such drastic measures have been taken and

that a civilised society has resorted to Frankenstein experiments with its feathered population is the cold harsh reality mankind has come to understand: no matter how much we kid ourselves, no one likes turkey. There's a reason why there's no such thing as a roast beef 'twizzler'. Even Bernard Matthews, the Michelangelo of fowl, nay the Mozart of mechanically recovered meat, knew his flightless muse was a, well . . . turkey. No wonder its name has come to be synonymous with career-wrecking theatrical flops and difficult second albums. No one wants to eat turkey for one meal, let alone breakfast, lunch and dinner for a period that straddles two different years (especially at Christmas 1999, when the turkey literally outlasted a millennium).

There's also no way to get turkey right. If your turkey is cooked badly, not only will it taste terrible and ruin your lunch, but you will also have to spend the rest of the day consoling your mother for having 'ruined Christmas'. If she cocks it up, the rest of the afternoon will be spent trying to retrieve her from a black hole of her own making, trying to cheer her up with pints of Baileys Irish Cream and *Gavin and Stacey* as she mopes from room to room flagellating herself with a sprig of rosemary, chanting, 'Shame, shame!'

The whole of my mother's Christmas hinges on that roast. She heaps so much pressure on it, and never seems to learn that none of us really care. We'd be happy if she served up a quiche with a sprig of holly in the middle. It's simply not that important. Don't get me wrong: roast potatoes are another matter entirely. She cocks those up, she's no mother of mine. But the turkey could be chargrilled in a bin fire and stuffed with gravel; with enough gravy I'd probably get it down and barely notice the difference. My mother is so keen to get it

right she's often resorted to experimentation. One year, she attempted to brine the turkey in her bath! To clarify: when I say her bath, she wasn't in it at the time. It wasn't bobbing around her like a giant headless version of a rubber duck. She'd read some Facebook post that claimed the best way to get that meat falling off the bone (as opposed to having to scrape it free like pebble-dash off an old terrace house, as per) was to give it an overnight soak in a tub full of salted water. So up she lugged her 8kg Kelly Bronze to the bathroom, lit some candles and drew it a bath. As it turned out, her chef cheat codes did work ... in a way. It was definitely more flavoursome, just perhaps wasn't the flavour she'd intended. Unfortunately, the bath's previous occupant had used quite a potent shower gel before running it for the turkey and some of the lotion had definitely clung to the porcelain, resulting in a Christmas dinner that had pretty hefty notes of lavender. No amount of cranberry sauce could conceal her mistake and she was so mortified she nearly locked herself in a cupboard till New Year. No matter how much we reassured her that every mouthful was (as promised on the shower gel packaging) revitalising. To compound matters, not only did the turkey taste of shower gel, but for the next couple of days my father definitely had a meaty bouquet after his morning bath. Not a surprise, given that he had essentially been bathing in jus. My mother had also failed, in her rush to towel down the bird and get it in the oven, to completely sweep the area. Daddy was not best pleased some days later to go rootling around behind the sink only to pull out a packet of giblets that had been lounging in the soap tray. All things considered, it was a very misguided experiment that has never been repeated. If you ever feel

obliged to cleanse your turkey before Christmas, I suggest taking it for a shower instead.

What makes this centrepiece even more problematic is that, even if by some minor miracle the cooking gods (Delia and Nigella) are looking down on you from their Aga in the sky and you do manage to pull off a successful roast turkey, it still has the capacity to ruin your lunch. You see, the problem with turkey is that it also provides the perfect fodder for another of Christmas's most tedious traditions: the dad joke. The poor creature has died not just for its meat, but to become the prop-cum-straight man for Britain's least-loved family entertainer. Yes, the moment that serving dish hits the table, it's like being transported back to the end of Blackpool Pier circa 1970.

'This bird's very plump. I've always liked a big bird; that's why I married your mother.' Genuine quote taken from one of our Christmas home videos, dialogue courtesy of Michael Whitehall, delivered to his infant children, aged four, three and one. Barnaby must be the only baby that learnt to roll his eyes before he could speak, so bombarded was he with Bernard Manning hand-me-downs.

'Does madam require stuffing?' is another in his repertoire, usually aimed in the direction of my listless mother, her spirit long since broken by years of this supposed humour. It is a joke Daddy once proudly told me he had purloined from a McGill postcard showing a randy butcher talking to a 'big-knockered' lady leaning over the counter, bought many years ago from the top shelf of a seaside news-agent's. Not a location, I pointed out, that many of the great comic minds went looking for their best material. I don't think Billy Connolly and Dave Allen were in there, looking

for some rock-solid gags to pick up as well as a windbreak and a crabbing bucket.

If you can get through the 'leg or breast man?' middle act of this pantomime of cringe, the finale is always the most tedious and protracted. A one-man parlour game in which your father sees how many times he can slip the word 'moist' into conversation before one of his family lobs a parsnip at his head. It's why – and this rule is becoming a bit of a recurring theme in this book – guests should be avoided at Christmas. The smaller the audience, the better; ideally it would be performed behind closed doors. I remember one terrible year when my sister thought it would be a good idea to invite her boyfriend round for Christmas Eve.

'You have met our family,' I cautioned.

But she wouldn't listen.

'Your relationship will be over by Boxing Day.' Maybe that was her plan all along – breaking up with someone can be a messy business. Easier just to introduce them to Daddy and let the rest take care of itself.

On the time scale, at least, I was proved wrong. As it turned out, it was doomed before he'd even got through the front door. The chap she was seeing at the time, sadly no longer with us – not dead, well ... dead to my sister, but alive as far as I'm aware – was a charming young man whose name I have omitted to save his blushes. Nice bloke, however – how can I put this kindly? – rather generously proportioned. Jolly! That's the nice way of saying it: he was jolly. Morbidly jolly. The sort of person who might want to consider having a band fitted to restrict themselves from further jollity. I only mention this as it's an important detail in the story. Molly had already prepped us to be on our best

behaviour but, unfortunately, when her beau arrived, she and I were on the top floor of the house. We were probably spying on my mother through the keyhole of her bedroom to see her sat astride the turkey rubbing things into its back in the manner of Daddy's Cambodian masseuse friend. When we heard the doorbell echo up the stairs, it was like everything went into slow motion. My sister darted from the room like the bionic woman charging down the stairs towards the front door, desperate to intercept the unwanted welcoming party. Unfortunately, she didn't quite make it. She arrived just in time to witness my father greet him. My dad, who by this point in the proceedings was pretty 'moistened' with sherry and who, I feel I should add, had never met this boy before in his life, opened the door, looked the portly teenager up and down and shouted through to the kitchen, 'Hilary, we're going to need a bigger turkey!'

I don't think Molly and the chap's relationship ever recovered, and certainly since then Christmas, like other holidays, has been an immediate-family-only affair. Like a pandemic – containment is the first priority.

Entertainment

Carol singers also get pretty short shrift. We used to have to practise drills as children for turning off the lights and hitting the deck when Daddy could hear the rattle of their charity buckets coming up the drive. The old miser would sooner set the dogs on them than be parted with his hard-earned cash. He's told me he's considered burying landmines under the porch. I think if he had his way, even Santa Claus himself wouldn't be welcome. Daddy's ideal Christmas

decorations would be a cattle-grid on the roof and a lit fire at the bottom of the chimney. The problem with our family at Christmas is that there are two very conflicting approaches: my father's, who makes Scrooge look like Richard Curtis, and the rest of the family's, who start playing Christmas songs in late October. I guess what I'm saying is that he's Michael Caine, and we're the Muppets.

Another bone of contention is the battle for control of the sound system. I personally like the pop classics: Wham!, Mariah, RuPaul's 'Hey Sis, It's Christmas', which my father once heard and nearly did a George Bailey over Putney Bridge (the words 'end of civilisation' were muttered more than once). And, of course, the timeless classic and possibly greatest song of all time: East 17's 'Stay Another Day'. How do you make a Tony Mortimer? Add two parts Lennon to one part McCartney and mix in an oversized white Puffa jacket. Garnish with sleigh bells and serve. Yes, mine is a playlist of wall-to-wall tinsel-tasselled bangers. Whitehall Senior, unfortunately, has a slightly more archaic ear and insists on stinking out the room with a load of old hymns and, worse still, monks singing plainchant! Oh yeah, nothing gets the Christmas party started like the sound of ten Friar Tucks warbling in an abbey. God knows what the neighbours think, probably that we've joined some sort of cult. The sad thing is that we can't even find a compromise.

'What about Michael Bublé, Daddy? Where do you stand on him?'

'His windpipe.'

What kind of a psychopath doesn't like Bublé at Christmas? Christmas without Michael Bublé is like a wedding without a cake or a christening without a baby. He's central to the

whole event. I reckon at some point in the mid-2000s we all unconsciously decided Michael Bublé was going to take the place of Jesus, and we were all fine with it.

The trick to winning the Battle of the Christmas Playlist with an elderly relative is to manoeuvre them incrementally. It's a war of attrition. Steal an inch here and there. You don't want to go from Bach to Bieber in one shuffle, else you could end up in tier-4 Classic FM lockdown. Instead, ease your grave dodgers into the twenty-first century with some old favourites: Andy Williams, Dean Martin and so forth. Thaw them out with a bit of Ol' Blue Eyes. Then, when they're giddy on Swoonatra, roll out a couple of gateway crooners: your Josh Grobans, your John Legends. Ease down the volume a little; they won't even realise they're no longer listening to Frank (if you've got the festive booze drip right, all of the sensory information they're getting should be pretty scrambled by now). Crank it up a little with a bit of Kelly Clarkson, maybe a dash of Disney. Then, when their guard's down, bam! Jonas Brothers' 'Like It's Christmas'! They won't know what's hit them. By Boxing Day, they'll be slut-dropping to Ariana on the kitchen table. Slowly, slowly catchy Grande.

I understand that, for parents, some traditions are hard to break with. My father is very set in his ways (almost literally fossilised) and, as with most things in his life, a bit of a snob. For my mother, the only thing that gives her more satisfaction at this time of year than the trip to the dump when it opens after Boxing Day is being able to bring Christmas in on budget, which to be fair to her is a monumental achievement when you are married to a man that lives his life like a minor royal. He may not give to the carol singers, but that's only

because he believes charity begins at home, specifically with the National Society for the Protection of Michael Whitehall from Pretty Much Any Discomfort. I remember one year, my mother took drastic measures to tighten the purse strings. I think it had been a hard year for the Whitehalls' finances: three sets of school fees to pay and offers to Daddy's main client and cash cow, Christopher Biggins, were drying up a bit (the emergence of respect for non-binary genders has been murder on the Widow Twankey set). So, Mother decided she was going to experiment with her sourcing of Christmas supplies to pinch the pennies. She knew my father would be apoplectic to learn anything he was consuming had not come from his supermarket of choice. (Waitrose, where else? He claims it's great value compared to the competition, by which he means Fortnum's.) So Mother got creative. A 'light' single-basket shop was done at Waitrose to make sure she had enough packaging available, but then there was a clandestine trip to a rival retailer in the dead of night to bulk up on actual supplies. It took all my energies to keep her deception a secret, as my father wolfed his way through an entire sleeve of mince pies, eulogising about them being the crustiest, most moreish pastry he'd ever eaten, crumbs tumbling down his chin.

'Good old Waitrose, you really can taste the difference!'

No, you can't, you fool. They're from Lidl! You're eating bargain-basement mince pies that your wife covertly trans-ferred into a Waitrose box as you were snoring in front of *The Weakest Link* Christmas special. Mutton dressed up so convincingly as lamb, not even a shepherd would spot it (I don't think there was actually mutton in the mince pies, but I wouldn't put anything past Lidl in their quest for customer

value). 'Where could this dastardly system lead to now it had been road-tested?' my frugal mother must have thought. The money she could save by decanting litres of Morrison's prosecco into an empty bottle of Perrier-Jouët from the year before. Her entire Christmas shopping could be transformed by two John Lewis bags and an afternoon in Sports Direct. Alas, the following year she was rumbled by an empty box of Poundland crackers at the bottom of the recycling bin. He nearly garrotted her with a miniature nail clipper. Fortunately, that was from Poundland too, so it broke in his hand before he could do any serious damage.

Decorations

The Christmas tree is another bone of contention for many a family. When is it acceptable for the tree to first appear and, more importantly, when has it outstayed its welcome? Personally, I like it up before the John Lewis advert first airs (although said premiere can lead to Daddy trashing the tree in an incandescent rage, depending on how much 'inclusivity' they've put in) and down around the time you break your dry January pledge, a date that can vary quite wildly. A couple of years ago I only got to 6 January before cracking, mainlining a jeroboam of rosé to myself like a cross between a vagrant and the Ghost of Christmas Present. I thought making it to the 6th was pretty pathetic, but in 2021 I only got to lunch on the first. The thing is, bringing a Christmas tree down is depressing, deforesting your good spirits and clearing a path back to reality, back to the long chew on the dry bone that is life. It's the comedown after what (depending on your family) has probably been a bit of a down

already. OK, maybe I'm being a little bleak, but surely it's something you'd want to delay as long as possible. My dad likes to get it up around Christmas Eve and have it down by the midday kick-off on Boxing Day. His problem, though, is that due to his advancing years, he can't completely have his own way, as he now struggles to get it up without assistance (I'm fighting every urge to make the joke I want to make here). We therefore have to find a happy medium, which tends to work out as some day in mid-December, when he finally breaks and allows us to decorate the tree.

Alas, this proves to be another merry activity he's able to strip the gaiety from like a health-and-safety officer at an orgy. DCI Dickhead of the Fun Police will stand in his dressing gown, doling out orders to his children and making sure the tree is decorated to his strict specifications: nothing too garish, everything symmetrical, homemade decorations we made in art class safely buried out of sight on the inner branches. All the while, my mother circles the base on her hands and knees, catching any loose needles in a dustpan and brush lest, heaven forbid, one sully her carpet. One year, I managed to sneak a Rasta Claus bauble onto one of the higher branches. It said, *Have an irie Christmas.* Oh, he wasn't happy at their Christmas drinks, when Mrs Worboys spotted it and asked why Santa Claus had a palm leaf printed on his sack. That ain't a palm leaf, Judith, that be some nutty skunk!

I will add for balance that my mother is the complete opposite and can get a little carried away with the pomp. She is obsessed with fairy lights. She will literally put them on everything: the tree, the banisters, any hanging light fixtures, around the cooker hood, in the bathrooms and even on both the dog and Winston. Last Christmas, she went as

far as decorating the whole front of our house in fairy lights, then insisted on staging a small ceremony to turn them on. I think, truth be told, she was a little peeved that her newfound minor stardom post-*Travels with My Mother*, sorry *Travels with My Father*, had coincided with a global pandemic and lockdowns. She'd really been angling for a panto season, I think; a couple of weeks in Great Yarmouth with Les Dennis and a Krankie. Worst-case scenario, she wanted to be asked to turn on the Christmas lights somewhere. She'd put out a few feelers in September to city councils, cold calling a few mayors, harassed some Twitter accounts and had some positive noises from the ones who didn't block her (when I say 'positive noises', I think they were just humouring the demented). But then, the coronavirus came along and scuppered her chance of landing the ultimate Z-list-celebrity status symbol (it's one rung up from appearing on *Pointless*). The nation's high streets went dark. Still, she wasn't going to let a global pandemic rain on her parade. If a Christmas lights ceremony wasn't going to come to her, she'd put one on herself, and that's exactly what she did. The family were rounded up and made to stand on the street below to await this fuse-box version of Trooping the Colour, in the freezing cold, shouting out a countdown as she ran around the house switching on all her fairy lights before emerging onto the balcony like Eva Perón, holding Winston and waving to the crowd, which consisted of her three children and one bemused dog walker, who must have thought it was the halfway house's annual Christmas do. Thank God, I was wearing a mask and therefore my identity remained anonymous (I don't know where Daddy was; he might have already locked himself in the wine cellar for the evening).

You may have seen her lights if you happened to have been on Google Earth last Christmas; it must have been a nice touch for the people on the International Space Station looking out of their window. Or perhaps they thought London was having a second Great Fire. The event was only soured a little by the fact that, the following day, one of the fairy lights went out and I was sent up a ladder to unplug and re-screw each light individually until I found the offending bulb. Next year I will pay a town to take her and Winston off my hands. Seriously, any councillors reading this, get in touch and name your price; the further away from London, the better. Do the Shetland Islands have a high street?

The upside of my mother's draining the National Grid for her Christmas lights display is that, at least, there is not enough power in our house for my father to put up an electrical perimeter fence around the presents. A measure, I have no doubt, he would take were it available to him. He takes the same attitude to the gifts under the tree as Donald Trump did to the Mexican border – none shall pass. He's almost certainly considered building a wall. My father, like patriarchs up and down the country, spends the weeks before the big day patrolling the base of that tree like a goose protecting its nest in hatching season, determined to make sure no one gets anywhere near any fun before the allotted time he has designated on his anal Christmas Day schedule. The schedule usually proscribes that no presents be opened until after he has cooked us all breakfast. That would not be so much of an issue were it not for the fact that my father is a challenging cook. It's not so much the quality of the food that he produces but the time it takes for him to churn out these simple dishes. How can it take a man half an hour to

cook an egg? What's he doing in there, laying it first? Let him loose with his wooden spoon and he is able to block the festive flow like a culinary embolism. Christmas morning is, in fact, the only morning of the year that my father suddenly decides he's going to roll up his sleeves and 'have a go' in the kitchen. When I say 'have a go': his repertoire is pretty limited. It's scrambled eggs on toast, or scrambled eggs next to a piece of toast. It is a dish he claims to have mastered by cooking the eggs entirely with residual heat. Therefore, what then ensues is his present-less children have to endure the most drawn-out process I have ever witnessed: a vast pan of a dozen freezing-cold eggs hovers about a foot above the smallest ring on the hob, which is pitifully flickering away without any danger of heating anything. He may as well be cooking them over a cigarette lighter or with his morning breath. It can literally take twenty minutes for them to even flirt with solidifying. Christmas morning is like a Chinese water torture, with him slowly stirring away as we sit agitatedly at the kitchen table, longingly eyeing up the spoils beneath the tree in the sitting room next door. Desperate for this festive filibuster to end.

'Any minute now these eggs will go, just got to be patient; cooking scrambled eggs is an art. It is the ultimate waiting game, children, you've just got to hold your nerve.'

Hold your nerve? It's breakfast, not *SAS: Who Dares Wins*. FOR FUCK'S SAKE, GET ON WITH IT!

One year, he stood at the stove for – I'm not exaggerating – half an hour before my mum came in and pointed out the hob wasn't even on. He'd literally been trying to cook them with room temperature. Maybe he was hoping climate change would eventually do the job for him.

Presents

In most families, the gifting timetable on Christmas Day is something different generations have very opposing views on. For the 'kids', it's a sprint. You want to open everything under the tree as though there were a meteorite heading towards your living room. As a child, I wanted a klaxon going off at around 6 a.m. and everything opened before the sun had bled through the curtains. Ideally, I'd have opened everything on Christmas Eve. For the adults, Christmas is a slow burn, a gentle meander. It's one of life's great mysteries, that shift in mentality; like how, one day in your mid-twenties, you suddenly wake up and like red wine. At what point in your life do you make the mental transition from wanting to open your Christmas presents the moment you get up to being perfectly content to drag it out for as long as possible? Some parents like several different sittings, interruptions for meals, black-and-white movies. If you've been born into one of these families, all I can suggest is throwing yourself on the mercy of the NSPCC. One year, my dad suggested opening the main presents *after* dinner; we looked at him like he'd just scraped Rudolph off the bonnet of his Mercedes. I am thirty-two years of age and proud to say that I am yet to reach that watershed moment when I can walk past a Christmas present and not want to tear it open. I'm still dreaming of that voice-changing Pink Power Ranger helmet; but I know the day will come, probably in some cruel twist of fate when I finally have kids of my own, so I can in turn torture them.

The best part of Christmas has always been the gifts for me, and by that I literally mean the gifts for me. I'm not one of these weird virtue-signalling saints who claim my

favourite part of Christmas is watching people's faces light up as they open the meticulously selected presents I have spent months agonising over. Is that the whiff of bullshit I smell? Christmas presents are like orgasms: anyone who claims it's better to give than to receive is a barefaced liar or has never received a proper one.

My mother is so of the opposing view that she even gets off on giving them out to strangers, the Mother Teresa of Putney spending her Christmas Eve at hospitals and home-less shelters dishing them out to the needy and deserving. Presents, I should clarify, not orgasms. She's a kind woman but even she has limits to her charity.

'Please, Hilary, you're only meant to be giving them soup!'

'I'm sorry, Muriel, I just thought he'd appreciate it on such a cold evening.'

I can't believe I just wrote that.

All of her priorities are on a different plane from mine at Christmas. When my father has passed out drunk on the sofa and I am finally let loose under the tree (probably shortly after 11 a.m.), I will rip open presents with all the grace of a randy teenager fumbling at a bra clasp. Opening them with my mum around is a far less enjoyable experience, as for her it's all about retaining and then smoothing the wrapping paper so she can reuse it, a measure that slightly defeats the purpose of wrapping them up in the first place. The whole point of wrapping them is for the giddy thrill of the rip open and reveal. Much of that excitement is lost when you have your eagle-eyed mother looming over you with a judgemental gaze, ironing board at the ready as you care-fully attempt to peel off a piece of Sellotape without taking any of the Santa Claus print with it. It's like bomb disposal.

The stress of opening them is matched only by the crush-ingness of the disappointment you feel when you finally get inside and realise that the gift you thought bore the exact dimensions of the new FIFA is actually just another unsold copy of your father's memoirs (the rent on that warehouse isn't getting any cheaper). How many Christmases can he get away with giving us all that book? Still, they came into their own during the pandemic toilet roll shortage.

I don't know why we bother wrapping presents, given my mother's obsession with recycling the paper. I mean, I think I do know actually: it's a chance for mothers the world over to have a wrapping paper flex. How are mothers so much better at wrapping up gifts compared to us mere mortals? Her gifts look like something you'd see in a shop window. Mine look like something I've just blown my nose into. When I cut a piece of wrapping paper, it looks like I've done so with a set of chopsticks. Witnessing my mum cut wrapping paper is balletic; it's like you're watching Torvill and Dean's Boléro. The grace, the sinuosity, the scissor glide; a manoeuvre only mothers have mastered. You try doing that and you'll end up with a butchered edge and a severed artery, and a piece of wrapping paper that is always less than half a centimetre too short for the thing you're wrapping. My mum takes one snip of the blades and she's off, sliding up that sheet of wrapping paper like a swan across a lake. In the time it takes me to find the end of the Sellotape by scraping my nail around the roll ten times, she's wrapped, tacked and stacked each gift with an individual bow that she's hand-ribboned with yet more scissor sorcery. It's like she's missed her role in life: she could be performing Caesarean sections – she'd do it in seconds, leave no scars and have all the stitches tied in a bow. What's

the point in me even trying? I might as well just shove my gifts in a plastic carrier bag and write the recipient's name on it with a Sharpie. Don't tear your carrier bag, Mummy, we can use it again. That's your Christmas bag for life. Daddy, your presents are in the Lidl bag. Thought you might enjoy reading your own memoirs again. Who doesn't love a re-gift?

What makes my mother's attention to detail when wrapping gifts all the more baffling is the beneficiary of her labours. Many moons ago, it used to be her beloved children that she doted upon and spoiled on Christmas Day, but since we have each in turn grown up and flown the nest, her attention has shifted and we are (to put it in the delicate language she uses) dead to her. Nowadays, my mother is no longer just my mother; she is, first and foremost, a dog mother and the apple of her eye is Filomena. She could not be more obsessed with this creature if she had breastfed it herself (and maybe she did; God knows what's happened in that house since I left). Mummy's Christmas is now entirely geared around her canine companion. She is obsessed with Filomena; mainly, as she is at pains to point out to us, because Filomena is the only one of her babies that 'didn't desert her'. By 'desert' I mean move out of the house when they become a grown adult. Many measures have been taken to ensure everyone is aware of Filomena's newfound status as favourite child. My old bedroom has been turned into a shrine to the dog: pictures of Filly on all of the walls, Filly dolls, cushions complete with slightly barbed idioms stitched on to them, like 'When I needed a hand, I found a paw'. But Christmas is when my mother is at her most crazed, in particular when it comes to the gifting. I don't know if there are other dog mothers who behave like mine, but my mother not only

buys gifts for the dog. She will also buy gifts for herself that she will wrap up and then pretend that the dog has given her! We all have to sit there on Christmas Day watching this ludicrous farce unfold and pretend that these are the actions of a rational human being and not of someone that needs psychiatric help. Watching her with the gifts she bought herself and wrapped herself, shaking them curiously next to her ear, 'Ooh, I wonder what Filly's bought Mummy?' Hopefully a straitjacket.

And the gifts she gets for this dog are ridiculous. It's so spoilt! The only presents I get from my mother now are passive-aggressive ones: deodorant, a net to catch my beard trimmings in, a babygrow.

'Mummy, I don't have a child.'

'Don't remind me.'

I don't know how she thinks the reproductive urge works, like I'll think, 'Oh, I seem to have acquired a lot of baby clothes. Maybe I should get a baby to go with them.' Instead of a babygrow, she'd be better off gifting me a broody woman with low standards.

Yet the gifts Filly is showered with are preposterous. Last year, she got artisan biscuits. My mother opened them up and talked Filly through the selection, like a waiter taking you through a tasting menu at a Michelin-starred restaurant. She even started asking the dog for feedback.

'Which biscuit did you prefer, Filly? The parmesan and rosemary or the winter truffle and black pepper?'

I sat there looking at her, thinking, 'Hilary, how refined a palate do you think Filly has? She didn't seem that fussy just now when she was outside on the towpath licking another dog's arsehole.'

Christmas Traditions

Filly is, of course, now included in the family Christmas card as well. My mother puts a little paw print at the bottom of the card, just below the forged signatures of me and my siblings (including the other usurper among us, Winston! Don't start me on him!). Although I'd have thought the neighbours don't so much want a card from Filly as a promise for her to stop shitting on their front doorsteps. For Christmas cards are another tradition my mother gets rather fixated on. Daddy would wall in the letter box on 1 December, leave it blocked throughout the festive period and knock it back through once the income tax deadline has passed. I witnessed a tremendous rant one year, when a handmade card came through the door that contained a load of glitter. He opened the envelope and it went off like a rainbow grenade, showering his crotch in sparkles and making him look very briefly like a furiously angry My Little Pony. From the noises emanating from the hallway, you would have thought he'd opened an envelope of anthrax. I came down to investigate the cause of the commotion to see him kicking the envelope into the front garden with a skid mark of glitter across the door mat behind him. It looked like he'd just murdered a fairy.

My mum, on the other hand, and much to his chagrin, *loves* a Christmas card. She takes great pride in the Whitehall Family Christmas card list, as if it was some elite group rather than a rogues' gallery of hangers-on, bores and weirdos. She'll often, rather arrogantly, commend newfound friends that have been added to it. Some of these 'friends' genuinely look honoured to have made their way onto this illustrious

list, and one never quite has the heart to tell them that it is literally one of the least exclusive clubs in existence, given that the criteria to join it are:

1. Have you ever had a conversation of more than a minute with my mother?

If the answer is 'Yes' you're on it. That's it. There are no other criteria. There are probably Amazon delivery drivers on my mother's list. There are definitely a couple of traffic wardens. She leaves them their cards under the windscreen wipers. I don't know how she has the time to write all of these letters. She must be outsourcing some of the work. There's probably a factory in Sri Lanka somewhere with an army of workers on minimum wage handwriting Christmas cards to the entire South of England Ladies Hockey League and to every attendee of Mummy's boot camp in Norfolk. She literally sends them to everyone and their dog, and I wish that phrase wasn't being used so literally: there has genuinely been correspondence from dog to dog. If I were the British Library, I wouldn't get too excited – I don't think these are letters that need to be preserved for the nation. My mother, naturally, also loves *receiving* a card, especially if it contains a round robin. She likes nothing more than tucking into a nice, long, gossipy essay, and the more banal the detail the better. In a world where we have more entertainment at our fingertips than ever before, Mummy would still rather read about how a distant cousin considered taking a summer holiday in France, but ultimately decided 'this wasn't the year for it'. She knows everything about her semi-literate former neighbours' offspring's very modest annual achievements

('Simon has advanced yet further up the management chain at Big Yellow Storage!') yet she still hasn't seen *The Sopranos*. What is she doing with her life? Sometimes she will go as far as to try to read them out to us, like we would be interested. No one wants to hear these letters; you'd be better off taking them down to the local hospital and seeing if they want to use them as anaesthetic. Thank Christ my father's normally able to head that one off at the pass. He is what you might call 'a tough crowd' for such material. He struggles to feign interest in his own children; what possibly makes her think he's going to want to listen to a three-page biography of our old cleaning lady's daughter?!

'I'm sure Shelia and her family had a very interesting 2020, Hilary, but unless it started with her miraculously turning into Alan Bennett, I don't want to read about it.'

At least by January, we are able to wean her off the Christmas cards with marmalade. Her marmalade-making madness begins the minute the tree has been deposited at the dump and lasts for only for a couple of weeks because, as she likes to remind us constantly, 'the Seville orange season is very short'. A tiny window to get the copious batches made and sent out as a follow-up gift to basically everyone on that Christmas card list as well.

It's often the Christmas holiday that crystallises quite how diverse the tastes of your family are. They say 'opposites attract' but I think it's truer to say 'opposites make you grateful to be back in your own home again, ideally by 27 December'. It's why television channels dedicate entire teams of people spending a full year trying to piece together three days' worth of schedules, and are still nowhere near cracking that nut,

'Something for the whole family to enjoy'. It's the Holy Grail. A feat that – in our family, at least – thus far has proved elusive. It's yet another area where tactful diplomacy and fragile compromises are the least dangerous route through. A negotiation resembling international treaty talks. Bringing peace to the Korean peninsula is less taxing than carving up the territory set forth in the double issue of the *Radio Times*.

'If you can watch *Call the Midwife* at seven-thirty, then I get *Naked Attraction* at ten o'clock.'

'Fine, I'll swap you a repeat of *To the Manor Born* for Gregg Wallace in a mince pie factory.'

'OK, if I watch *Mrs Brown's Boys* then—'

'I'll take an Uber home and never see you again?'

And so it goes on. Mummy ends up having to watch *Naked Attraction* on catch-up.

The problem is, even if you do manage to wrestle control of the remote, you still have to watch the programme you chose with an unwanted running commentary.

'Comedy died with Morecambe and Wise,' comes a voice from an armchair into your right ear.

Not entirely an unexpected opinion to have for someone of my father's generation. An opinion I wouldn't have minded him sharing were it not for the fact that what prompted him to share it was watching the Christmas special of *Bad Education*.

'Well, two million people beg to differ, Daddy.'

'Ha! Two million! Did you know that 180 million people tuned in to watch the Morecambe and Wise Christmas special of 1970?'

'Yes, Daddy, because the only other option in 1970 to watching it was looking out of the window.'

'Good idea. Let me know when this drivel is over.'

To him, everything about Christmas was better 'back in day': the movies, the TV, the songs. About the only thing in his mind that has maintained its integrity in Christmas's unseemly transition from religious festival to carousel of commercialism is the Queen's speech. He talks about past speeches the way people reminisce about the end of *Breaking Bad* (and this despite the fact that she always says the same thing – I'm pretty sure she freshens up the desk photos more frequently than her bantz). The last great bastion of British exceptionalism, imperialist porn, the biggest television event in the OAP calendar, it's like the *Love Island* final for the elderly and vulnerable. I cannot articulate enough how big a deal the Queen's speech is for my dad. One pretty clear indicator is that we are made to stand for its entire duration. Yes, you read that right, not just for the national anthem (which would be mental anyway as we are in our own living room watching a TV) but for the entirety of the broadcast. This has happened for as long as I can remember; actually, even from before I can remember: there is a home video of my first Christmas as a baby with Michael jokingly lifting me by the arms so that baby-me respected his monarch. Thank goodness social services never got their hands on that piece of evidence. I suspect that, in years to come, the boot may be on the other foot. If my father's health were ever to take a drastic decline, I know the instructions would be that, even if he's bedbound, I am to get out the pulleys and winches to have him on his feet for that speech. It will be in the instructions just below the bit about making sure Hilary doesn't try to sign over anything in his will to Filomena.

Christmas Abroad

For all that's been said, my very particular (some might say peculiar) Whitehall Christmas came to a grinding halt in 2020. Instead of being back home with my mum and dad in Putney, for the first time in thirty-two years I spent Christmas on the other side of the world in a hotel room. And lo and behold, I realised how important a family Christmas was to me. I didn't even need three ghosts to visit me in the night. As I lay there in the bathtub of the hotel, slowly beginning to prune, still struggling to digest the room service 'turkey club' – which I'm afraid to report was far from moist – and pumped up the volume of my *Call Me Irresponsible* album in the hope it might drown out the tears, I realised even a festive Bublé bath wasn't going to help me get over how much I missed Christmas with my family. How much I missed every grand tradition, every silly detail, everything I would usually complain about: the turkey tantrums; the slow-cooked scrambled eggs; the waking up with back

ache because I've had to sleep on a rock-hard mattress on the floor of my father's study; having to pretend I enjoy some weird, old red wine he's been hoarding in the cellar and that's now so far past its best, so full of sediment it's like it's being drunk from an ashtray; the three-day debate about whether to have Christmas lunch or dinner, knowing full well it will end up being 'lunch' around five o'clock, after which no one feels like eating another meal for a fortnight; being forced to write a thank-you letter as a grown man to an uncle I don't really like for a can of Lynx Africa; the endless discussions about bin day. It's the holiday that, perhaps, I malign more

than any other but the one I didn't know how much I missed until it was taken away. I, like so many others, would only come to realise that in the year they cancelled Christmas. So I would like to say: make the most of Christmas with your family while you can because, pandemics aside, there will eventually come a day when you'll be carving the turkey and there won't be a nasal drawl at the other end of the table pumping out double entendres like they hadn't long gone out of fashion, and your mother's thrifty madness will be a distant memory. Celebrate their eccentricities while you can, bite your lip when they ask if the woke police will arrest them for singing 'White Christmas'. Never take that time for granted. 'Tis the season to be jolly lucky you have that bunch of weirdos in your life, even Filomena.

Conclusion

WELL, THERE YOU HAVE IT; I hope you were all taking notes. If, having read all of that, you feel more prepared for your next family holiday, then I did my job. If it's terrified you so much that you're considering changing your name and going off-grid to avoid ever spending another second with them, again in the long term you may come to thank me. I certainly hope that by drawing back the veil and sharing with you some of my family's intimate secrets, our catalogue of cultural misdemeanours and a few sins of the flesh, you might now look at your own nearest and dearest and think, 'You know what, actually you lot really aren't that bad after all.' Yes, you and your mother might have a complex relationship, but at least you've never shared a naked sauna with her; of course your dad can be a bit old-fashioned, but he's never spent any of your inheritance on memorabilia that could be seized by the FBI.

The reality is that whatever lessons you may have learnt from the Whitehall Odyssey (a working title for this book that was rejected on grounds of pretension), no matter how much you try to prepare, the one thing you can guarantee from a family holiday is that it is going to throw up some unexpected surprises. There will be cringe-inducing moments, faux pas you didn't think even they were capable of committing, missed flights, lost bags, baffled customs officials, friends estranged, restaurants left under a cloud of ignominy. But would you have it any other way? My dispatches from the frontline should remind you not just that you are not alone, but also that as stressful as they are, the family holiday is always worth it in the end. It will provide memories that last a lifetime, even if some of those memories could more technically be categorised as emotional scars. They will provide stories that you will be regaling people with at dinner parties or stand-up comedy tours for years to come. And there will be a treasure trove of photographs, many of which will haunt you till the day you die. I will come clean: the presence of some of these images is the reason my mother has negotiated quite such a significant position in regards to any profits this book might make – she's got more incriminating photographs than the entire Getty archive. You think the photos you've seen in this book are bad, imagine the ones we vetoed!

If you are a younger reader and have been reading this book from the midst of the madness, try to see the bigger picture. Maybe you're on holiday now, taking refuge in these pages while locked away in the toilet of a Starbucks in Alicante as your father tries to haggle down the price of a frappuccino. Try to laugh or else you'll cry, be as patient as

you can and, above all, remember to be thankful: there was a time when we had to do all of this without a mobile phone for company. Let that sink in for a minute. Just you and your family in a villa with no YouTube or social media. If you wanted to unload you had to do so into a diary. A diary that in my case my mother would later edit and redact.

To any older readers who might have reached the end of this book and felt a pang of sadness at having reached the end of this trip down memory, I will remind you it doesn't have to be the end.

When, aged twenty-eight, I decided I was going to roll back the years, ignore my better judgement and the advice of my acting agent and dive back into holidaying with my family for a second time, there was a large part of me thinking. 'What the hell have I done?' As it turned out, it was one of the best decisions of my life. It's not lost on me how lucky I am to have had such a rich second act to my family life. I've got the chance to make a fresh set of memories with my mum and dad, and spend time with them again as adults. I got to know them all over again, often in ways that proved to be a little bit disturbing. But I have no regrets; OK, maybe some yoga-based regrets.

So I say to you: throw caution to the wind. I've armed you with all the knowledge you need – every tip, cheat code and cautionary tale – to feel like you can safely say it's time to get the band back together for one last gig. You may have a young family of your own now and be umming and ahhing about whether bringing your parents along with you is additional childcare or really just additional children to care for. But come on, what's the worst that could happen? It's time to live a little.

Tell Dad to blow the cobwebs off the cluster of padlocks that protect that pension pot, inform Mum that she's going to need to get some new swimwear that's more appropriate for a woman of her age, and round up any siblings that still speak to you for that family holiday finale that could prove to be either a celebrated comeback tour or a franchise-ending sequel. Only time will tell.

Whatever you decide, make sure you have my words ringing in your ears. Don't fall for the villa with the sea view, never touch a monk's head, always carry wet wipes and please, for the love of God, avoid the andouillette sausage.

About the Authors

Jack Whitehall is an award-winning comedian, actor, presenter and writer, widely celebrated for five series of his hit show *Travels with my Father* on Netflix, and writing and starring in three series of *Bad Education* for the BBC, playing Paul Pennyfeather in Evelyn Waugh's *Decline and Fall* also for the BBC, and creating the character of JP in the award-winning Fresh Meat for Channel 4.

A regular team member on eight series of Sky One's *A League of Their Own*, he has appeared three times on the Royal Variety Performance, including becoming the youngest ever host in 2015, and has also hosted the prestigious BRIT Awards for the last three years.

An acclaimed comedian, in 2019/20 Jack toured his fifth and biggest ever stand-up show around arenas in the UK, Australia and Dubai, which was also filmed for Netflix.

In addition, last year saw Jack co-star in the Disney film

Jungle Cruise alongside Dwayne 'The Rock' Johnson and Emily Blunt, as well as starring in Paramount's *Clifford the Big Red Dog*. He has also just finished filming *Robots*, in which he plays the lead opposite Shailene Woodley and he is about to start filming for season two of Apple's *The Afterparty*.

This is his second book collaboration with his father Michael, following on from *Him & Me*.

Michael Whitehall was a leading theatrical agent and producer whose clients included Daniel Day Lewis, Edward Fox, Judi Dench and Colin Firth. He produced *The Good Guys*, *Noah's Ark* and *Element of Doubt* for ITV, as well as numerous theatrical productions around the UK and in the West End.

Michael appeared with Jack on their show *Backchat* for the BBC, and subsequently five series of *Travels with My Father* for Netflix. A regular guest in Dictionary Corner on Channel 4's *Countdown*, he also co-hosted *Hard to Please OAPs* for ITV as well as appearing on *Celebrity Gogglebox for Stand Up to Cancer* with Jack and Hilary.

His books include *Shark Infested Waters*, *Backing into the Spotlight* and *Him & Me*, co-authored with Jack.

Hilary Whitehall. Daughter, sister, wife, mother and recent grandmother. When not busy attending to the various needs of members of her family, she occasionally manages to work as an actress (*Fierce Creatures*, *The Bill*, *Woof*, *Miranda* and *Bad Education*) and is also a photographer.